Hose the House Down

HOSE THE HOUSE DOWN

STORIES OF INSPIRATION FOR WHEN YOUR LIFE IS FALLING APART AROUND YOU

ARACELI VASQUEZ

KB
Khrusos Books

Austin, TX, USA

Published 2022

ISBN: 979-8-9863421-1-5 (Paperback)

ISBN: 979-8-9863421-0-8 (eBook)

DISCLAIMER

Neither the author nor the publisher assumes any responsibility for
errors, omissions, or contrary interpretations of the subject matter
herein. Any perceived slight of any individual or organization is purely
unintentional. The events and conversations in this book have been set
down from memory to the best of the author's ability, although some
names and details have been changed to protect the privacy of
individuals and referenced parties.

Brand and product names are trademarks or registered trademarks of
their respective owners.

To my daughters. At times, life may seem unbearable.
Know that there is always a way out.
Una puerta, ventana, agujero de raton pero siempre hay una
salida.

CONTENTS

From the Editor   ix
Preface   xiii
Introduction   xvii

1. Step Not Given   1
2. Roller Coaster Ride   11
3. Fool Myself Once   27
4. Merry-Go-Round   45
5. Stop the Merry-Go-Round   53
6. Find Your Life Vest   63
7. Emerge   77
8. Non-judgmental Heart   89
9. Chain Link   107
10. Breaking Off or Tightening the Link   127
11. Happy Times   143
12. Reflections   151

Acknowledgments   155
About the Author   157

FROM THE EDITOR

"Even when it's not pretty or perfect. Even when it's more real than you want it to be. Your story is what you have, what you will always have. It is something to own."

— MICHELLE OBAMA

As an editor and writing partner, I find this quote inspiring because it is a reminder that each book is not just a collection of words, but the culmination of a life. It isn't always the "perfect" story. It doesn't always have the most "perfect" words (assuming we humor the notion that perfection can actually be attained). Instead it is the unique viewpoint through which we get to see the world as someone else has lived in and learned from it.

Hose the House Down is a title I feel privileged to have supported because of the way the author takes ownership of her story. Part memoir and part self-empowerment, this book provides a taste of what it's like to experience abusive relationships and find the strength to leave. What makes this narrative so compelling for me is that it doesn't focus on the pain and struggle, but rather a mother's efforts to save her daughter who's stuck in a trap the mother knows all too well. There is not one storyline happening here, but two: The author's mission to save her daughter, and the author's own reconciliation of generational wounds stemming from the relationship she had with her own mother and men.

If anyone were to ask me what this book is about, I would say on the surface it's about escaping a crisis, but beneath that (and hopefully not too far down) it's about becoming resilient, women supporting women, and ending dangerous cycles through honesty and vulnerability. Araceli is a force to be reckoned with as a mother. As an author, she is honest, hilarious, and at times a little cut throat—all of which are qualities she's adopted over many years. And in her pages, you see one unmistakable constant through-line: love. This is a book about love.

Abuse is a difficult topic to capture in a book for many reasons. Chiefly, it can be so hard to write about without slipping and tumbling into flashbacks and discomfort. In addition, it can be hard to write the stories for an audience whose never experienced it to be able to understand and connect with—or without sending an audience who can relate back into their own trauma. Araceli's approach is to share her story in tandem with her daughters to give readers a way to explore difficult moments while anchoring in something that is a bit more tender.

As a final note about the text, I will say while some moments may seem hilarious and others unbelievable, the important thing is not whether one can actually believe what happened. What's important is seeing how each moment fits together. You can't take this book for any part by itself. The story uses a series of layers stories and intentionally nonlinear storytelling to bring to light awareness of events and valuable takeaways. I don't always feel driven to leave an editorial note like this, but this book is an exception because I find myself not only moved by the stories and inspired by the key figures, but motivated to understand the complex effects of domestic abuse and generational trauma. I think anyone truly reading this book would have the same inclinations by the end.

—Andrae Smith, Jr.

PREFACE

People who know me have called me a warrior among warriors. I don't know that I would put myself on a pedestal, but I always find strength and drive when I see people being victimized. This may be because I know what it feels like to be subjected to physical and verbal abuse. Still, I believe it's a part of my calling to help others stand up for themselves and what is right. This is something I'm stubborn about because I've had to find this strength in myself.

September 16, 1982, it had been raining for three days in Brownville, Texas. I remember leaving the house with books and shoes above our heads, wearing trash bags like ponchos. (Let me tell you, poor people have solutions to everything. We did our best to shimmy along the chain link fence to the end of the alley to avoid getting our clothes wet or getting cut by broken glass hidden in the water that had flooded the land around the house.

When my brothers and I left for school that morning, the water had risen so high, it was already threatening to enter and flood the house. By midday, I kept calling home to see if our home was okay or if my mom was awake. Mom had worked all night long the night before, and when she arrived home, I knew she was dead tired. It was around three in the afternoon when she finally picked up the phone, and all I remember was hearing her feet splashing through the water.

"The house is underwater!" She shouted.

"You have to turn off the electricity!" I told her.

I left school immediately and began to race home. I didn't even know why we were still in school when half of our neighborhoods were flooded. I was sure my mom didn't turn off the power because she woke up to this nightmare, but it was a wonder the city hadn't shut off the power for safety.

I arrived to find my mom sitting, defeated, on a chair in the middle of the dining area, crying. "I'm cursed!" she kept saying. It was also the first anniversary of my dad's death, so you can imagine her state. Just as she was saying this—and it's funny the things we remember—a knot from the wood flood (machimbre, she would call it) shot up into the air from the water pressure. At that point, we had an indoor fountain.

When my brothers arrived, I directed them through as many activities as possible to save our house. First, we brought in cinder blocks to raise the furniture as high as possible. We (finally) turned off the electricity.

Then, we put all the important things we could remember on top of the furniture. Meanwhile, my mom was still in her chair. In all the time that I had known her, I had never seen my mom break down like this. I had to keep going to her, placing my hands on her shoulders and telling her, "we are alive. It's going to be okay. We're all okay."

Eventually, we couldn't do anything else, and we left to take refuge at our high school. The entire community of Southmost, where we lived, and the neighboring areas were forced to evacuate to this make-shift shelter. I remember seeing the aerial shots from when the news copters flew over. It's still amazing that nobody died.

Once the water started to subside, the Red Cross rolled in with cleaning supplies and aid. I was very active with the Red Cross to communicate and translate during this time. This was incredibly important because We were a poor Hispanic community, and most people were uneducated. At the time, the workers with Red Cross were mostly English-only speakers.

Unfortunately, the damage was unbelievable. We needed more aid, but FEMA was the only way to get funds and support. You will read more about this story in Chapter 9 of the book, but I want to point out that this was when the mayor of our city did not support the people. Instead, he blamed us for the destruction. Getting the help we needed became a fight, and I did not back away. This work was too important. In our culture at the time, women were supposed to be meek, docile, and ignorant, yet there I was, standing up to the challenges. And as you'll learn, my stance got results.

You may be wondering why I've chosen to open with this. It is one of the earliest instances of me finding and showing my strength in a crisis. As you will get to know, through peeks into my past throughout this book, I've been in many crises. I didn't know the strength I had in some of them, but I became good at surviving.

This is where I gained the perspective I needed to be able to write this book someday. There will always be challenges in life. Some are more desperate than others. Some will make you question yourself, and you'll need to find the strength you didn't know you had, but if my story comes to be any example, I want to tell you that when you find your strength, don't let it go. And don't be afraid to use it.

My strength helped me protect my family and make important changes time and again. Mine. A woman's. Even when everyone around me showed and told me what a woman's place is supposed to be, I found my strength and now have the voice to write. By sharing the stories and conversations in this book, I hope that I can empower other women like me to be strong. They are already strong, even if men (and sometimes other women) tell them they shouldn't be.

Introduction

The day I returned to the United States, my insides churned with nerves from when I got out of bed until my flight touched down at Austin Bergstrom Airport close to ten at night. I landed on June 13, 2020, amid COVID-19 protocol and just after several Black Lives Matter rallies—two of many reasons I had chosen to keep my distance from the U.S. for so long. I was returning for the sake of my daughter, Maxi. Call it mother's intuition, but my instincts had been telling me for the past year that she needed me. Her sisters had confirmed as much in a few phone calls.

Her marriage to her husband (who we called "Sissy Boy") was challenging to say the least. For the sake of his privacy, I won't disclose his name. I thought it would be appropriate to call him that while writing because that is still how I see him after the events that transpired, but my editor suggested I at least give him a name. So I may call him Egorr or Sissy Boy interchangeably.

My last visit with them had been over a year prior, in the summer of 2019, and he sat there talking on and on about how Maxi had gotten fat and lazy. So, of course, I gave him a piece of my mind. (What mother wouldn't?) It was clear what kind of man Egorr was and how precarious a situation they were in, but Maxi wanted to stay for some reason. My instinct said "abuse," but I always respected her wishes to sort it out as her own woman. Now, after months of prodding and reaching out to her from my home in Jeju-Do, Korea, I had gotten through, and she finally began to tell me what was really going on. My heart ached, and I knew my time abroad was over.

I sat outside the airport with five suitcases and wearing a dog carrier, wondering not, "What's taking the driver so long?" but "Why did Maxi love him?" Did she still love him like she had when they married, or was she hanging on, as many women do, because society is so unkind to divorced women? Was that the reason she was putting up with so much?

My driver arrived right when my dog decided to pee on me. I should have let her out of the carrier, but my mind had been so fixed on my daughter that I neglected my other baby girl, Opal, a four-pound Maltese that had filled my life with joy for the past two years. I quickly wiped my shirt as best as I could and then got into the white Van.

As we drove through the downtown area of Austin,

my heart sank. I knew things had been bad in the United States, but this? I blinked several times, using part of my face mask to wipe a couple of tears as we passed worn-down neighborhoods and boarded up stores covered with graffiti. Apparently, the rallies had gotten out of control, and some folks started smashing storefront windows.

"Oh my goodness! I did not expect it to be this bad," I said.

It had been well over seven years since I left to teach abroad, and I could see myself retiring out of the country. This dismal scene confirmed why I felt I no longer belonged. If it were not for my daughters, I would have turned around. However, this was—they were—more important.

After two weeks in quarantine, I finally got to visit Maxi and Sissy Boy, and he really lived up to the nickname. He belittled her and complained that she wouldn't clean up or do as he said. Every time I heard him talk this way, I found myself sizing him up, thinking, "Could I knock his teeth out?" He was only five and a half feet tall, skinny, and balding.

"Do you even love my girl?" I said.

"I guess." He bobbed his head and shrugged.

"You guess? You either love her, or you don't ."

"Well, of course, I married her," he said. His voice had a hint of a laugh in it. You know that tone a teenager gets when they are not taking you seriously.

"So what, Egorr? Now, after eight years, you decide she's too fat. She's too lazy. She's too sickly. Do you even hear yourself?" I said. "I told you my daughter was not the type to be super clean. I warned you, and what did you say? 'I love her, and that does not matter. I can clean too.' I told you she was sickly, and you said, 'I'll take care of her. I do that with a sickly brother, so I'm used to that.' Now it's a problem?"

He was sitting across from me, holding a picture in his hand. He held it up close to my face. "Look, she was not as fat as she is now! You need to tell her to clean up and lose weight!"

At that moment, I knew my daughter was in a crisis. This boy had no respect for her. There was no way their marriage was healthy—in fact, it was dead, and Maxi had to know it. She always said she could read him like a book, that he could not lie. Yet here she was trying to lie to herself. Why?

There is more to this story that I will reveal in the chapters to come, but I want to say here is I know why this bird stayed in her cage. I was her once. (It's ironic how patterns repeat across generations despite our best parental efforts.) She may not have realized it yet, but she was stuck because she had lost sight of her worth. He had pushed it down so far that she did not know what she deserved. She was also confused. How could the man she loved be so cruel? What changed? It did not seem real. There had to be hope.

After going through my share of bad marriages, I knew her struggle. It's one that I see way too often repeating in young women around the world because they don't know how or when to stand up. As a mom, I look at young people like my daughter. I think about what I saw driving back from the airport, and I feel like that chaos reflects what's going on in our homes behind closed doors. People who don't heal go on to cause harm. (As much as I hate to say it, this includes Egorr.)

I decided to write this book because it's time to start healing. I think about what I went through and what my daughter went through. I was able to help her, but many young women don't get a true mama bear protecting them. There are many who, for varying circumstances, are unable to reach out to their moms. This book is for them.

In the coming chapters, I will share stories from Maxi's life and my own in hopes that it can help you, my readers, not feel so ashamed of or stuck in your situations. I know first-hand what it's like to be in abusive relationships and come under attack by shame, loneliness, anxiety, fear, despair, and self-loathing. If you are in an abusive situation, these mixed emotions will keep you from moving forward and becoming a strong, self-assured person.

When we face what feel like insurmountable problems in life, we tend to retreat inward, becoming buried by these feelings. You need to know that shame and loneliness are ways that our minds tell us that we may need to seek help. Seeking support for myself is something I've had to learn to do and not be ashamed of. I need you to know that you can do this too.

You are not alone if you're reading it now as a parent

or survivor. You can find kind-hearted individuals who have likely gone through something similar within your community- your neighborhood, friends, and family. Letting go of shame is hard, but there's nothing you should be ashamed of. I know, it's easier said than done. I'm not saying it won't be hard; it will likely be one of the hardest things you do in life. I am saying I believe in you. You can learn to navigate those hard life situations and come out feeling stronger and quite proud of your accomplishments.

Chapter 1

Step Not Given

Egorr was the son of a Naval officer and a Spaniard woman who was a real "witch" (I'm sure you know the word I'd like to say). Throughout my lifetime, I've dealt with military families. In some of them, like Egorr's, cleaning becomes an obsession, sometimes creating rifts in the family because it's not normal to be so tidy. The military husbands often don't receive proper mental care and develop abusive tendencies.

I don't say that to belittle service members. I bring it up only because so many of my friends have gone through this, and even divorcing was difficult, if not dangerous. I've unfortunately also witnessed how the children of such families don't fare well either. They tend to carry on some of those obsessive and abusive patterns into their relationships, and I feared this would be the case with Egorr even before he married Maxi. But they were young and in love, and I respected Maxi's wishes.

I snatched the photo from Sissy Boy but did not bother looking at it. "To me, she looks the same. She may be five or six pounds heavier, but she's the same person. Now you, you seem to be balding. How will you fix that? My daughter married you with a full set of hair."

It was obvious he was looking for a way out. He gave some cocky lines about how men lose their hair and how it should not be a problem. I called b.s.

This whole time, Maxi acted like she did not hear us or just was not interested. Finally, her attention shifted, and I told them, "If you are planning on divorcing, just do it. Talk it out, make decisions, and do it. Stop all this drama."

Maxi stood up and walked outside to the back patio to smoke. She left the door slightly cracked, and I could hear her crying in our silence. Maxi, crying? She had always been my tough girl, my "I won't take shit" girl. Now, all I could see was a woman who had been beaten down.

I went on scolding him. You're probably thinking, "is this whole book going to be about the author yelling at her son-in-law?" No! I promise it's not, but this moment was so critical. It was obvious that Egorr was checked out. He did not want to be married to my daughter, but instead of stepping up like a man, he just beat her down and strung her along as if there was any hope left. And Maxi was going along with it, stuck between love and pain.

It can be hard to accept when a marriage is failing, even when the signs are there. The mixed feelings that come and go daily seem to keep us from truly focusing on the problems plaguing the marriage. Denial comes around when you see a glimpse of hope. It's that tiny lie we tell ourselves when we see that our partners have done one small thing that pleases us. We start to think, "maybe he is changing…" "he is trying…" "he does care…" and even "maybe I'm being too unreasonable."

Then we top it off with the worst lie of all: "it's worth giving him one more chance." We tend to lose count of the amount of "chances" we give abusers. We want to be the kind and understanding person because if we keep feeding them kindness, maybe, just maybe, they will change how they see us and give us what we need. You probably know what happens. Same old same old. Denial keeps this loop open. Meanwhile, friends notice we are changing and ask if anything is wrong with us, and along comes good old shame.

Shame comes in because a part of us knows we're not alright, but we don't want anyone to know we are in an abusive situation. How could we have fallen so far and allowed this to happen? They would think we are weak and incapable of taking care of ourselves. On the other side of the coin, we start saying things like, "I don't want to burden anyone with my problems." We begin to self-isolate for two reasons:

(1) Because we want to keep hope alive. No one wants the story where it ends badly, and that's just it. Our hearts deeply fear that kind of suffering.

(2) Because the part of us that knows the truth (there

is always a part of us that knows) is terrified of the scorn or judgment we might get for our lives being so bad. So even when people just want to help, it feels like pity.

I believe that this is due to the unkind society we live in. Words like issues, toxic, broken, difficult, and who knows how many more are out there, keep us in our self-made mental jail. So we keep taking the abuse because our minds have worked out that it is less dangerous than what others will say and make us feel. All the while, our abusers get to go on draining our self-worth like taking a rolling pin to a sponge until we just feel unlovable. This is the most dangerous part because everything just feels numb, and the only question is, what would be the point of trying to leave?

I sometimes wonder how much of this was true for Maxi by the time I got there. After a few minutes, she entered the room, listening intently to what I was telling him, how a real man would not do what he was doing. How it was shameful, and he was being a sissy boy. How if he were trying to get one over on my daughter, I would be all over him. She smirked a little, like a child watching their bully get scolded.

I looked at her and said, "Maxi, I want you to know that I'm very disappointed in you. How could you allow this man to treat you this way?" Her smirk vanished, and her body seemed to stiffen up. Her eyes searched for an acceptable answer, or perhaps somewhere to run and hide. I realized instantly I had probably said the very thing she feared the entire time, so I quickly added, "I also want you to know that I'm here for you. You are not alone in all this."

She wiped tears from her red, puffy face. "I felt so alone for years, mom. His family keeps butting in. They tell me how fat I am and how dark I am. The mother is Spaniard, and she's racist."

She sounded like a child tattling, but I was proud and relieved. Finally, she had the guts to speak up in front of Egorr. While I was abroad, it had become difficult to get ahold of Maxi, and when we could talk on video, she was always somewhere dark in what looked to me like the bathroom. Eventually, she confessed that he did not like when she talked to me, so she tried to hide it. I could still see and hear the fear in her, but at least at this moment, she was strong enough to speak up.

"You two are feminazis!" he said, stumping out of the room.

My girl sat next to me and hugged me. "Mom, I'm so glad you are here. Just having you back makes me feel stronger."

I hugged her back. "I'm here for you, Mika, and whatever you need to do to get this situation dealt with, I will support you."

"I love him, mom... I want this marriage to work."

There it was—the seesaw moment. If you don't know what I'm talking about, this is the point when it seems like someone is on the verge of leaving a toxic situation. They have gained a little ground in reclaiming their personal strength, but they've not come far enough to see that it is time to let go. They get a temporary lift, but they fall back down again. At some point, they have to get off the ride.

It was so obvious to all of us that Sissy Boy wanted out, but she was clinging to him. There was nothing that she could do to make him want to stay, which created so much resentment. I know because this is one of those moments where patterns repeat. I had done the same with the love of my life, Gee.

Gee had bright blue eyes that shone when he smiled. His smile... I can't count how many times I thought I might faint when I saw it. I was in that heart-pounding butterflies-in-my stomach type of love and was eager to please him because I thought he felt the same way.

Gee was not my first love. He entered my life over two years after my second divorce. I was determined to stay single at the time, but God (I thought it was God) had other plans. Gee was the type of man that knew how to treat his lady. Always brought me flowers. Treated my girls with what I thought was true fatherly love. He never forgot a birthday, an anniversary, or a holiday. He was that too-good-to-be-true type of man that, these days, makes us cautious. But what were the odds that someone so good could be bad?

As far as I'm concerned, my third marriage was the only marriage that had truly mattered in my life. It was the fairytale story all girls dream of. So that's why it hurt so much when it ended.

We lived together in a beautiful two-story home on

top of a hill. I had built two ponds, one at the bottom of the hill and one at the top. Out back, we had an acre of land with well over one hundred Texas trees, and the girls had the perfect treehouse with a loft. I was so happy for so long. But, more importantly, my girls were happy, and they had everything they'd ever want.

Then, one day, I woke up unable to bend my right index finger. It was swollen and throbbing like I had slammed it in a door. Within weeks, I went from a "normal" healthy person to needing a lot of attention and help just to live. I was in pain, and doctors pumped me with so much medication it all but ruined my body. My clothing size jumped from a women's three to fourteen within months. Finally, doctors diagnosed me with SLE Lupus, an autoimmune disease that took everything from me.

Supporting me was hard on Gee; I knew it. I wanted my life back and believed that I could get it once I was better. Then, after eight years of marriage (three of which were plagued with my hospitalizations), Gee decided to tell me he was gay. He would have to divorce me because he was no longer happy. "Betrayed" and "blindsided" seem like the only words to fit what I felt, but they are not strong enough. They were underpinned by this sense of being unworthy and having failed, even though I knew it wasn't my fault. There are so many people like me who suffer from an autoimmune disease and are left to deal with it all alone. Everyone leaves sickly.

Now, I saw Maxi's marriage at the same spot mine was when Gee walked out on us. Egorr had the same countenance that Gee had, present but distant, cold as if part of him had checked out a long time ago. Deep down inside, I knew Egorr was likely to leave her when she least expected it because she was truly in love with this man, just like I had been in love with Gee. It was going to devastate a part of her. I knew I couldn't stop it, but I would be here for her, so she did not have to do this on her own as I had.

———

Late in the evening, I finally drove home. It was a long one-and-a-half-hour ride that I did not mind making. It gave me room to think through things, to focus on how to help my daughter. I saw myself in her, the scared young lady unsure of her future. When Gee and I divorced, he married one month later. Meanwhile, I had doubted every step of the proceedings. Not knowing how I would make ends meet terrified me.

There was little support for divorced women. Women did not support each other either. My family—my mother, brothers, and sisters—already labeled me a whore for having two divorces. Hispanic culture was lagging seriously behind in protecting their daughters. I had a lot of reasons to doubt myself and doubt that it was real. I was on the seesaw, even as life was happening.

Maybe this is where I had failed Maxi. I knew that my girls were embarrassed about the number of divorces I had. This may have been another reason Maxi was attached to making it work. So she would not end up like me. As a mother, I wish I could have protected them from that, but sometimes life has its own plans.

I knew the road ahead with Maxi would be a tough one. I knew that she'd question everything and anything from her upbringing to the tiniest event in her life. This included looking at every aspect of me as a mother. These were the same things I had done. It was a long process that had to happen. It would have to happen again, but I had tools in my bag to help her out this time.

I had an insatiable thirst for knowledge back in the day, which led me to try becoming a Psychologist when I was in college. I had taken most of the courses, but when I started the counseling course, I realized it was not for me. Listening to the experiences of others who had been abused was still too triggering for me. None of those credit hours went to waste, though. I had learned many things that would help me navigate motherhood and other areas of my life. Now, it was time to pass on my knowledge. It would be a long gut-wrenching journey for both of us as she navigated this life change. I had also to prepare my mental self to accept and respect her decision no matter what that was.

I drove up my driveway, got out of the car, and locked my door. It was a hot summer evening, and the stars were shining. I heard Opal's faint squeaky bark as I walked up to the house.

I opened the front door and knelt to greet her. "Where's my beautiful girl?" I said.

CHAPTER 2

ROLLER COASTER RIDE

Sometimes when we are in painful and confusing situations, as Maxi was, we want to crawl into a small hole and hide from everything and everyone. It's like the world keeps closing in around you. That small dark hole is the only place you feel intact, but you have to shrink down so small that you forget yourself to fit. I was not about to allow Maxi to do that. I knew that the best way to help another woman out when in crisis was to keep calling. Keep showing up for her.

We live in a culture where everyone wants to mind their own business and keep their heads down. The thing about abuse victims is that they keep their heads down, hoping someone else will speak up. They may not even know that they are hoping for it because they are so confused or brainwashed, but that is when the heart is most needed. That's what I wish my sisters would have done, and that's how healthy relationships are fostered.

Maxi and I talked on the phone every day, sometimes for hours, after that incident. I also showed up at her house on several occasions because I was "in the area." I made it a point to know where she was at all times. Some call it overprotective, but this helped me ensure that she was doing well and safe. It also helped her feel the support she needed during this crisis period.

On some days, she would tell me how hopeful she was for her marriage and wanted to have a future with Sissy Boy. He would do one tiny thing or praise her once in a while, and she would take that as a sign that he might change back to the man she married, the man she thought truly loved her. I kept my reservations.

To be honest, I always had them. Egorr wanted to marry her after they had dated for just a month. He was twirling a red flag over his head like the color guard in a high school band. We knew nothing about him or his family, but she said yes. I allowed it and wondered ever since whether I should have been more protective then. The more Maxi revealed, the worse their story got. It came out he had been accused of rape in college. Rape. After eight years, I could see clearly just the sort of person my daughter was married to.

Egorr also had a daughter. It slipped out after they had announced their engagement, and when we asked about it, he brushed it off as one of those "mistakes" he made when he was young and did not know better. During their marriage, I met his daughter once over the internet and once in person for maybe thirty minutes during the summer break. I did not attempt to get close to her because I had gone abroad and did not want to form an attachment since she was only with them over holidays and some summers. Now that the marriage was likely over, I was not about to make an effort to make that connection.

On one particular day, I was going over to Maxi's, and it seemed likely that I would bump into her because she was there for the summer. Maxi told me not to worry because Egorr and his daughter would spend the day at his parents' house. I arrived, and the house was somewhat clean. Maxi's rheumatology kept her from doing more, but she was trying.

"How are things going?" I asked as she gave me a cold bottle of water. The Texas heat was no joke, and I could not stop the sweat, even with the AC on full blast.

"I don't know, mom. I'm not even sure how to tell you this."

"Just say it, Mija. There's nothing under this sun that I have not heard or seen before." I said.

"It's not about me," she said, wringing her hands.

"Did something happen to your stepdaughter?" I asked, watching Maxi's body for signs of truth.

Maxi's stepdaughter was a pre-teen and had started menstruating the summer before. She was beginning to "develop," and Maxi had to have the talk about taking care of her body and all that goes along with a girl getting her period. I hate to use the wording "young lady" because it implies, at least in my estimation, that the child is ready to marry.

"I think there's something really wrong with Egorr. My stepdaughter was in the shower with the door closed, and he walked in on her."

I nearly choked.

"She yelled at him to get out, and you won't believe what he said."

I did not have to believe anything. Intuition was always there.

"She was covering herself up with a towel, and he told her, 'I'm your father, I'm allowed to see you naked or whichever way. You don't need to cover up anything.'"

Then Maxi broke down and told me about how he had a problem with porn and masturbation. He would do it when he was supposed to be working upstairs, so she tried to keep her stepdaughter downstairs. She told me how he would sit her on his lap and get hard-ons. His only excuse was that he was sick and working on getting better, but he never went to see a counselor. He was sick, but not how he was trying to spin it! She told me there was another incident with a teenage girl in Austin that he was worried about. His family was able to make that one "disappear."

As I said, I had no trouble believing any of it, but that did not stop my insides from burning. This guy was touching children. Even when you know someone is pretty much a dirtbag, you don't want to think they are capable of something so heinous and disgusting. Even I had a little more hope for Sissy Boy than that.

We talked for a long time. I assured Maxi that she did the right thing by educating her stepdaughter about her body and inappropriate touches. She was right to call out her husband's behavior and try to shield the child from that. Unfortunately, I told her, there are men out there who like to prey on children like this. They do these things and don't see the problem with it, and if we are not vigilant, those children are stuck living with PTSD for a large portion of their lives.

In a world that values or devalues women by their bodies' appeal and usefulness to men, this behavior makes it especially hard on young girls. Their approval in society is based on their sex appeal. They can sometimes feel more valuable because a man has an interest in them, even though the child in them knows something is very wrong. Many young girls (and boys, too) grow up with confused ideas about their bodies, boundaries, and worth because they are robbed of these things so young.

In this case, it was only more challenging because Sissy Boy's family knew he had a problem and was willing to cover for him rather than make him get help and protect this child. So I said it would be best to tell her stepdaughter about who she could talk to and how—teachers, counselors, us—if things got worse and she felt unsafe.

"Mom, I love him, and I want to help him," she said after a while.

I could not believe my ears. My Maxi was truly blinded. I took a deep breath and closed my eyes to feign thinking. Really, I was making sure I would not lose it and yell at her. What the hell was she thinking? Help him? She had to know there was next to nothing she could do for him. That's what I wanted to say, but I knew better.

"I don't want you to stress out about this," she said, "It's my problem, and I know I need to figure it out. I was afraid this would trigger your PTSD. I'm sorry I brought it up." She was trying to put the genie back in the bottle.

"Mija," I said with a calm but shaky voice, "I'm concerned for your stepdaughter. You know I will have to report this. I don't want to lose my teaching license. More importantly, it's the right thing to do. This may be a Godsend if you want to help both of them, but my priority is the safety of your stepdaughter. When does she go back to her house?" I asked.

Then, as if on cue, Sissy Boy walked in with his daughter. My eyes met his, and I wished for a moment that mine could shoot arrows.

"Hey, hey," he said. That was his typical way of saying hello. "I thought you'd be gone by now." He tapped his daughter's back. "Go upstairs and play with your dolls. I don't want you to learn from this feminazi." He never broke his gaze.

My heart pumped adrenaline through every inch of me. I learned early on that there were times to step aside and times when you would have to stand and fight. This was a plant your feet and grit your teeth moment. It was partly my own experience with childhood sexual abuse and partly my instinct as a mother, but I could not let him get away with this. There were now two beautiful flowers wilting because of him.

"No. I might stay here a few nights to make sure the gals in this house are respected," I said.

No. The one word that men like this can't seem to understand. It's easy to ignore when it comes from just one person, especially when you've already beaten them down or manipulated them for so long. But when enough people say it, things start to change. When I went through my experiences, my "no" was lonely because, as I said, there was not a lot of support for women in those days. So it was not likely true, and if it was, it was my fault for being too "loose" or perhaps just too pretty.

This time, things would be different. I told him before I would always be there for my daughter. As mothers, we have to do this. We have to be there for our daughters, sisters, and nieces. We are the only ones who can hold the line that makes "no" powerful against narcissistic men like Sissy Boy. When we don't, that is when trauma happens that often can't be reversed. Mine made me stronger, but that's not always the case. Some girls break. My daughter was breaking, and I had to share my strength.

He looked at both of us, thinking Maxi would back him up. But she was stronger this time, and it was more important than her fear of stirring the pot. When you suffer from abuse, stirring the pot is the last thing you don't want to do because you're just trying to survive, but if you don't stir it, sometimes it boils over and sets the house on fire. So it was time to stir.

"Oh, more of the feminazi bullshit." He rolled his eyes. "Maxi is exaggerating things. I did not see my daughter or stare at her. I needed things from the bathroom. Besides, I don't see why it's a problem if I see her naked. I'm her father. It's not like I haven't seen all that before." He pointed at Maxi's body. "At least my daughter is not fat like Maxi."

There it was again, calling my daughter fat. He truly did not love her. Why was she putting up with him? Why did she allow this? I knew, of course, it was her fragile mental state being young, confused, and belittled. I went off. If I told you everything I said to him that day, you would think I'm crazy.

I do want to tell you something about the world, though. Women always look crazy after they've been pushed too far. But no one ever challenges the pusher. He called me a feminazi, but I am proud to wear that title. It's not an insult. It's just a word thrown around by immature men who like women to be submissive and can't handle when we lift our voices. They think we hate men when really, we just choose to love ourselves too much to be stepped on or let anyone else be stepped on.

When a mother grizzly bear senses a threat to her cubs, she attacks and keeps attacking until the threat is eliminated. It seems crazy to us, but for her, perhaps it stems from the daily fear that some larger male will decide her cubs are a meal. Or that some human hunter will see them as a prize. This is why we now respect mother grizzlies as the embodiment of strength. At the very least, we know better than trying to come between her and her cubs.

Sissy Boy and I argued until I threatened to call the police. He had threatened me. He had threatened the girls. I could not reach my phone fast enough, but Maxi stopped me.

"Mom, please stop. This is why I did not want to tell you anything. Just leave. You are making things worse." Again, I could not believe my ears.

"Maxi. Really? Do you hear yourself? Do you understand what you're doing by giving him what he wants right now? You need to open your eyes, or you're going to wind up charged with harboring a pedophile."

Maxi walked outside to smoke. The fighting was too much for her nerves, and perhaps something else was breaking through for her. He stayed in the living room, and I stood in the kitchen.

After a couple of minutes, he entered the kitchen with a childish smirk like he had won something. "You know, Maxi will do as I tell her. I know she loves me no matter what."

What was this, a cartoon? I imagined a corny cartoon villain twirling his mustache, so certain that no one could stop him. He had no idea that I had opened the back door slightly while his back was turned away from me. I knew he was going to try me, and I wanted Maxi to hear every bit of the real person he was.

"Have I told you I bought a gun?" he asked?

What a pathetic power flex. A boy with a gun is still a boy. A bully with a weapon is still a bully.

"I'm not saying anything. I was just trying to be nice and make conversation." He said.

"Sure you were. Just like I was just calling the cops to come on over so they can sort all this mess out."

We were quiet for a minute, and then I finally asked, "When are you planning to leave Maxi? You are not fooling me one bit."

Nothing.

"Well, where's your conversation Sissy Boy? I know who your attorney is." I lied.

"Yes, alright. I have an attorney, and I'll make sure Maxi is left on the streets with nothing! She deserves nothing!"

While my face was hot with anger, I felt proud at the same time. I had him where I wanted him. Maxi had heard all of it. When she came inside, her face was plain, but the energy coming from her felt deadly. This was a pure betrayal. The insults were one thing, but a divorce? Leaving her with nothing? That could not be left alone.

To that point, I had never seen so much strength in her. He told her to keep her voice down. She would not. He tried to talk around it. She heard enough. She was, as I thought, finally seeing him for what he was.

Egorr gave some weak-hearted explanation that his attorney advised taking time apart to sort things out. He was considering going back to his parents' house after his daughter left. This was the first intelligent thing he had said and maybe the only opportunity I would get to dislodge her from his grip, so I spoke up before she could try to beg him to stay (one of the real "crazy" things we do when attached to our abusers).

"I think that's a wonderful idea. Most marriage counselors would push a couple to try out separation before making such a big decision as is divorce. I'm sure now that Sissy Boy does have good intentions. Maxi, this might be a good thing. You get to think things out and work on yourself while he does the same. If one of you feels this won't work after a month or two, well, then you two can come together and work on an amicable divorce. I'm sure that's what that attorney of yours wants, right?"

I lied like I never have before—and I would do it again to save my girl. She was caught in his lies, and I knew in my heart that if she did not separate from this man, she would become another murdered wife. She agreed to it, somewhat hesitantly, though.

"Once your daughter leaves, you can go to your parents' home. We will go to counseling to work on the marriage, right?" she said with hope in her voice.

As hard as it is to believe, this is how bad it can be. When a narcissist gets into someone's mind, it can be hard for the abused to escape. She held onto the little hope she had that their marriage had something to save, even knowing what he said. As a mom, I was proud of her progress but so hurt by the seesaw. Someday the ride has to stop.

I knew exactly the game this man was playing with my daughter. He was lying through and through. I sensed he was already paying up an attorney so he could hide as many of the assets as possible before he filed. Now that there would be a separation, I would have to deal with the fallout once my daughter was served. I did not understand why she kept on believing him. Realizing he would sleep downstairs and Maxi and her stepdaughter would sleep upstairs, I decided to sleep on the living room couch. Their bedroom was downstairs, and the living room was adjacent to the stairs. If he tried anything, I'd be right there. I did not sleep an ounce that night.

Early the next morning, I woke up and ordered breakfast. Unfortunately, the kitchen was a mess, and I did not want to clean it up.

"Mom, how did you do it?" Maxi asked me. "I mean, you went through three divorces. I can't be as strong as you have been. I don't want to be like you."

"Well, Mija, it was not easy. I did exactly as you are doing. If you mean you don't want to end up with three divorces, and I can see why you feel that way. The good thing, Maxi, is you don't have children with this man. You two are still young, and you can either work things out or move on to a better tomorrow."

She didn't say anything.

"It won't be easy, but it will make you a stronger woman. All of life's trials and tribulations tend to do that to us. Since I was six years old, I've had to be quite strong. It took me years to be able to stand up to abuse. I was not born strong; I had to become strong to deal with life. Plus, I had you girls to think about." I winked at her and gave a small smile.

"But mom, why did you divorce so many times? You are a wonderful person."

"Well, Maxi, all I'll tell you right this moment is that it takes two to make things work, but it only takes one to fuck things up. You cannot force the other person to be mature, caring, sensible, or loving. The one takeaway that I learned from all my divorces. That was my first major takeaway. The other one was that jumping into a relationship quickly is not the way to go. That was my mistake with the second marriage. Well, in the first marriage, I was only seventeen years old dating a twenty-four-year-old man." I got up to get more coffee.

"Ok, mom. I'm so happy you are here. I feel stronger just having you around," she said.

"I know, Mija. I know it might feel like you are drowning, but you won't. Before you know it, you will be smiling and happy again. It takes time, but first things first. Which taquito do you want to eat?" I smiled, pointing to the food.

I stayed until Maxi had eaten, and after a while, I decided it was safe to leave. The drive back home was tough after staying awake all night. Finally, I got home and jumped in bed with Opal. I slept most of the day and called Maxi as soon as I woke up.

"Mom, he came back and took his things and left without even saying a word to me." Egorr had taken his daughter home and was expected to stay at the house with Maxi at least another night. "He left me a note saying he decided to go ahead and move out early. His mom came for him because I need the car for my doctor appointments." She started crying again.

"Do you want me to come on over?" I asked. "No, mom. I need time to think. I'll call you later." She said between sniffles.

"Ok, Mija, if you don't call me, I will call you, and if you don't answer, I'm coming over. I love you, Mija," I said.

"Ok, mom. I love you too."

Like I said, showing up is important. Unfortunately, this is the part many of us get wrong. We tend to see someone in crisis, and we leave. We excuse our behavior by saying we don't want drama or we have our own problems. It's understandable, but if we don't show up for our own children, our own family, then it's no wonder they are so messed up. So, as a reader, I want to ask you, who do you show up for? I was determined to anchor my Maxi and be there through thick and thin. She had just received yet another punch in the gut, and I felt it.

I can't say I was happy that he had left because there was nothing to be happy about. Ending a marriage is not a fun, happy moment. It's devastating to everyone involved, but sometimes there's no other solution. My girl was hurting, and though I knew she would be a stronger person once she sorted things out, I knew the pain that she was enduring—the doubt. The uncertainty breakups can bring us. I saw myself in her. Now, we would have more time to have heart-to-heart conversations. I had to make sure my girl did not end up falling into a depressive mood that would likely further blind her. It was time to lift my girl up.

CHAPTER 3

FOOL MYSELF ONCE

I can't tell you how often I've heard men and women tell me things like, "I should have seen it, I should have seen the signs," and more. We all want to believe the person we married truly has the same kind of love we have for them. Maxi was still in that phase. You likely know the one I'm talking about. We hope for the best outcome, believing that things can work out—even when it's obvious to everyone around us that this will be a train wreck. We keep fooling ourselves.

Weeks passed since Sissy Boy, Egorr, went to live with his parents. Maxi was still hopeful that he was going to see a counselor. If he was seeing any counselor, it must have been from a far distance because I knew that narcissists like him see nothing wrong with their behavior. They shift blame and are unwilling to see their mistakes and grow from them.

On the other hand, my daughter had been seeing a

counselor virtually, and he was amazing with her. He kept trying to get her to see that maybe this marriage was over and she was in an abusive relationship. Slowly, Maxi began to shift her perspective, self-esteem, and insecurities, and so began the healing process. But like in many love stories that fall apart, sometimes we fool ourselves into thinking that maybe things will go back to the loving relationship we fell in love with.

"Mom, what happened in your first marriage?" she asked. "I want to understand why you divorced so many times." So there it was... All I could do was be truthful.

As much as we want to hide in that little hole where no one knows our truths or our pasts, sometimes being open is the best thing we can do. Share your truths without worrying about the judgment of others. This was one of those moments where my Maxi had to see me be vulnerable because it's something I had to learn, just like her. It was time to open up and share the life they knew very little about with my girl. It was time to show my wounds, the ones I'd been healing since before she was born, so she could see that she should not be ashamed of her current open wounds. When we are in crisis, we tend to feel as if everyone judges us. This is why it's good to talk, something society isn't doing much lately. So we talked.

"Well, Mija, I was barely seventeen, and things at home were horrible. You know how your grandma was. Rage was her sidekick. It had been well over a year since my dad died from cancer, and mom was taking out all her frustration on us kids. That belt would come out over any little thing. At times, it came out, and we didn't even understand why. I met my first husband when I was barely fourteen. He was twenty."

"Uhhh," Maxi made a gagging sound into the phone.

At least we were able to laugh a little. It was time.

My first husband had that look—dark, tall, handsome, with that Mexican mustache. I was too young to understand that one must look deeper than just looks. Anyhow, we met at my job. At that time, I worked at Denny's restaurant as a waitress. My mom had signed some papers to allow me to work. I'd sign all my measly checks over to her, but I liked the job because I'd hide some of the tips from her to have money for myself.

Every summer for at least two years or maybe three, I'd go to Denny's to work. We were boyfriend and girlfriend in hiding for a while, until close to sixteen. I finally told my mom I had a boyfriend. That was super weird. She met him, and of course, she did not like him. We rarely went on dates, and if we did, I had to have one or two of my brothers with me. It was a weird dating situation, and to be honest, I never really knew him until after I married him.

How that marriage came about was quite unusual too. I was so eager to get out of the house from under my mother that I planned to elope. My mother found out, of course. She and one of my older brothers forced this huge Mexican-style wedding on me. They gave me the whole, "It's what mom wants for you... You should do as you are told... Don't fight this. Just do it." Honestly, it was sickening.

I had proposed to my mother that I wanted to go to the Army. That got me a whipping like never before. I went to get my physical and was about to sign when I chickened out. I should have signed, but I had this desire for my mom to feel proud of me and how things were at home. Getting married was the only route left. Even college was out of the question. She'd say things like, "A woman is to be a housewife, not running around in offices where they end up becoming whores." It was quite different back in the 80s, and women were not treated as human beings, just people poppers with a broom. At least that's the way a lot of us felt.

I said this to Maxi, and she laughed. I thought I would dread telling my girls about this part of my life. Even though I knew it would come up, and I was very confident in who I'd become, I still hoped my girls would not hate me as a mom. Maxi asked why I did not just join the Army.

After being in JROTC for four years, going off to the Army would have been a better choice because college was not something I knew much about. Plus, back then, I was very meek and sort of quiet. I hid all my pain with laughter and that sort of thing. I was not equipped to truly think things through. In my family, we were not sat down to have real conversations about the possibilities for our lives. At least we girls were not. The opportunities that did exist were mostly for the "men." Marriage was the way out, I thought.

I saw marriage as the worst situation possible, but it seemed there were no other choices left for me to get the hell out. I saw how men cheated on women openly, and beat them up. It was a different world. So, since all other doors had closed on me, I figured I'd just marry and get out. Maybe I could make things work with this man. So, I got married. Never once did I truly look at this man and his behavior. After all, the only time I could see or be with him was at work or on the porch at home. It was not until I was 'engaged' that I was allowed to go out with him alone.

"Quite a shitty way of letting your daughters figure life out, don't you think?" I asked.

"I can't imagine living that way!"

The first year was the honeymoon stage, with all of the cute looks and cringy stories you hope your parents never tell you. But I told her. We could not keep our hands off of each other. We'd go at it on the stove, on the floor, in the shower, you name it. We were two horny young adults. I was barely eighteen for a couple of months when the wedding happened. I graduated high school as a married woman.

"Can you imagine that now?" I asked, making sure she was paying attention. She needed to see how different things were from how they had been brought up. Then, maybe she would begin to appreciate those differences.

At that time, at least where I was from, women were

expected to have a baby within the first year. It was barely a year when I finally got pregnant. I was so happy knowing I would have my child. This was how things were back then, and I dreamed of having a happy family. It never crossed my mind that I might have been too young.

The day my oldest was born was one of the happiest in my life. I gave birth in a clinic with a midwife. I was hoping for a girl, and there she was with that jet black hair to her shoulders and the most beautiful curls. The midwife commented on how long her hair was, and it looked as if someone had combed it to one side. Just perfect. That's when I learned a mother's heart is owned by her children. No questions about it. As I glanced over to my husband, he made his way out of the room.

That was the last time I saw him for the next three or four days. His family made it a big deal that he was having a baby and counting on a boy. By having a girl, I had somehow ruined everything. From that point forward, he treated me like a lepra. He avoided me and stayed out for days at a time. I tried everything to win his affection, but he never once touched me after my daughter was born.

Then he began to say that she was not his daughter. But, of course, he knew better than that. She looked exactly like him as a baby. (Thank GOD she looks more like our side of the family now!) That's when I learned men could flip. Soon after, I learned men like him used to belittle and discredit a woman before either leaving her or killing her. Yes, it was the thing.

My first husband used to tell me stories he'd heard of how to get rid of bodies by placing a body in a barrel full of acid. The other way was the Rio Grande River. Rumor had it there were so many bodies dumped there, you'd better not jump in, or one might grab you and pull you under. I'll never know if it was just talk or if he was considering it, but I'm glad to have never found out.

Looking back, there were serious red flags throughout our marriage. I got my first taste of real trouble with my husband when I was about six months pregnant. He took me to a bar that his friend's dad owned. In that bar, I learned who this man was. As soon as we were inside, several men left. Then the doors were locked. My young ignorance told me they were likely closing up the bar. Oh, boy! Was I ever wrong about it? My husband was playing a really dangerous game that many play in those parts of Texas. So, a gun was pulled out by one man and placed on the table. Then they began talking about me. One of them asked if I could be trusted. My husband said, "She can be. She's with me, and I guarantee she won't talk. She knows what could happen to her or her family."

The fear of imminent danger began inching from my toes to my head. I sat down at a table away from that gun and the men. Then they began talking about cars that they were waiting to hear from. The one man with the gun was "El Jefe." The boss. From what I could gather that day, there were at least three cars full of marijuana or cocaine that were supposed to go through the checkpoint in Sarita. One of the men pulled out some cocaine and began cutting and snorting it. Then I saw my husband do the same. My body felt suddenly cold, like the room had siphoned the warmth from my skin. My stomach clenched as if I might vomit. Who were these people?

After that day, he became increasingly bold, extending his trips to different parts of Texas and later all the way to New York. He'd bring cash back for them on planes by wrapping the bills to his body. He'd work for himself and his growing addiction to cocaine. Then, slowly but surely, his true colors came out. Abusers never show you their true selves while they are trying to get you into a marriage or a long-term relationship. It's like my mom used to say in Spanish, "Brand new vase, where should I showcase you, old vase where should I throw you or hide you?" It was her way of saying once the honeymoon phase was over, you'd see your husband for who he really was.

As time went on, his boldness was no longer confined to his "business." He began to accuse me of things like sleeping around. At first, I was sort of happy he was jealous because my child-like brain was not aware of the danger I was in. In my mind, it assured me he loved me, but I did not see that this was the wrong type of love—if you can call it that. That sort of behavior is typical of abusers. By the time I had the baby, It was easy for him to shape-shift into a monster. (Really, it was there the whole time.) He laid hands on me three times.

The first time, he slapped me and pushed me to the floor. The force of his shin against my ribcage pushed out all of the air from my lungs. My arms went up instinctively to protect my face. Even back then, though, I was no damsel in distress. When it dawned on me that this man was beating me, I got angry. I reached to my foot, removed one of my high heels, and began swinging. I must have hit him a dozing times until I felt the shoe connect with something hard.

"Fuck!" he said. He stopped kicking me, and I got up.

Our daughter was barely a couple of months old then.

The second time, he shoved me down to the floor again, but this time, he got on top of me and slapped me several times. I used my long nails to scratch him anywhere I could. He finally got off of me. The baby was three months old.

After her first-year party, he decided he'd try to choke me. That night, he came home very late. It must have been like two or three in the morning. I was sound asleep with the baby next to me. I woke up with his crushing hands around my neck and my lungs burning from lack of oxygen.

Somehow my little one-hundred-pound oxygen-starved body was able to push this man off the bed. He slumped over and began vomiting. Air rushed into my body. I was dizzy, but all I cared about at that precise instant was running from him. I grabbed my crying baby and locked myself in the bathroom. I must have spent something like twelve hours in that tiny bathroom waiting for him to leave again.

When I told Maxi this story, she was anxious to know where my family was. What had become of my sisters?

My brothers? My mother, even? She didn't understand why I was alone.

I had been telling my mom that he had been slapping me around, but she always replied with, "You chose him and married him, so now you have to put up with him. Marriage is forever," and "You must have done something wrong."

My sisters weren't any more helpful. When I saw them, they always made snide comments about how pathetic I looked or how pitiful my clothing was. It didn't help that during those years, I didn't know them at all. They'd left home when I was a toddler. They only knew whatever my mom would tell them about me.

I did walk to my mom's house, and I showed her my neck after my husband tried to choke me. When she saw the bruises, she agreed the violence was getting out of hand and let me move back home. It was a big shame and disgrace on her, though, and she made sure I knew it. My mother did not allow me to stay in the house. Instead, she gave me room in this "shack" behind the house.

I lived with my family for a few miserable months before I had saved enough money to move out. When I say miserable, I mean inhumane and just awful. You know, I wasn't even allowed in the house to shower, so I had to grab buckets and wash right outside the door of the shack. I'd use the door to block the neighbors from seeing what I was doing. It was messy and dehumanizing but bearable... until that winter.

The shack did have electricity, so I bought a tiny

single-burner electric stove. I used it to keep the place warm and to boil water which I'd pour into the bucket to bathe. I'd quickly wash my hair, and then I'd use a cloth to wash my body. When that water hit my scalp, it would feel like sharp needles. I did not care, though. I did not care how hard it was to try and find work while at the same time trying to hide from this abusive man. All I knew was that I had to keep my baby safe. I had no idea how to go about divorcing him, but I knew I had to move so he would not find me. I feared that he'd come in with his Mafia buddies and shoot everyone. Fortunately, nothing like that happened, and God sent angels to look after me. (I'll come to this in a moment.)

Fortunately, I still had a few friends at the restaurant. One of them was some big wig guy in the Housing Authority program. Apparently, he'd heard that I was having housing issues and asked for my address. He took me aside and said to me, "It looks like you are starving or something. Are you okay?" He was my first angel. I told him I was okay, but I needed to put money together so my daughter and I could maybe find a room or a place that was cheap enough to rent.

He told me about his program, and I felt a lump building in my throat. I had no idea at the time there were programs that would help people like me. He asked me to give him my address, and I explained how I was living in the shack behind the family house. He shook his head and heaved a sigh. His eyes were glossy, and his eyebrows were low. My story must have truly moved him because the next thing I knew, I was approved to move into an apartment on an emergency basis. Thank God.

I had no car, no savings, and had no idea how to get a restraining order. Friends from work helped me move out. Of course, it was at that point that I began looking at college. I was set to go to college, and this first angel had told me I would likely qualify for financial aid. That was my first big life shift and a life lesson.

Life has a way of giving us the lesson we need. What I learned from that marriage was not to believe anything men tell me but to pay attention to what they do. I also learned that some men don't like to lose. My husband wouldn't touch me while we were together. After I left, he found me and forced himself on me many times. Finally, when I was truly fed up, I had the guts to start the divorce procedures. The first step was to file for child support with the Attorney General's Office. I started there, and I didn't stop until I had finalized divorce papers in hand.

———

"So, why the second divorce from Papi? Maxi inquired

"Well, you were a baby when I first lived with my second husband. Your sister was barely three by then. I watched how he treated you girls and fell in love with him for being a good father figure."

After my first divorce and the verbal abuse from my family, I married the next man that came around and treated me decently. I did watch for any signs of abuse, and after living together for about a year and a half, I thought it was safe to say I had found the perfect man. He was much older than me, but I did not mind. We eloped, and I truly believed this would be a happily ever after. When you're young, that's how you see relationships. You find happiness and think it will be forever. Forever is a conception of the young.

A few months into our marriage, I was finishing my second year in college and would receive my Associate's degree. It was the proudest I had ever been. No woman in my family had ever gone to college. I was working at the District Attorney's Office and started doing well for myself. I had good insurance, good pay, and a wonderful boss. Sometimes I wonder if I should have just stayed there until I fully finished college, but I was always looking to better myself financially, so I could give my girls a better life than I had.

Unfortunately, there was a reason I was the first woman in my family to go. In Hispanic families, this wasn't how women were supposed to spend their time. We had responsibilities and duties to our families and to our husbands. Even though I was doing well and contributing to the household, his family didn't like me. They told me I was not paying enough attention to him and that my job was not to get educated but to be home raising my kids.

"If he leaves you for another woman, then it's your fault," his mother said during one incident. "You're not tending to him as he deserves." Around that same time, I started getting calls from someone claiming to be his mistress. (Of course, he denied it.)

By that point, my husband had decided he could not work. He had diabetes and spent most days in bed. I hired a lady to come to clean the house and take care of the girls while I was working and paying for his car. He was like my chauffeur, dropping me off at work and later at school. If I were paying more attention or a little less trusting, I would have realized that was just another way for men to keep track of women. The funny thing is, it's always men with the biggest trust issues who try to control the women in their life.

Right before Thanksgiving break, one of the investigators from the DA's office came to me with some binoculars. You see, my husband's parents had a house just two blocks from the office, and I was on the third floor.

"She's there with him right now. We are leaving early. If you walk there, you can catch him in the act." He urged me to look from the top window that faced toward his parent's house.

With binoculars in hand, I got up from my desk. This had to be a joke. But the way my skin was crawling, I knew this had to be it. I got to the window, held the binoculars to my eyes, and looked at my in-laws' house. There was my husband's car. Next to it was another car I didn't know. That bitch, I thought.

I had forgiven him so many times. I had chosen to believe him so many times. We had fought, but I thought by being faithful and bringing in the money, I could somehow make it all better. (The things we are willing to put up with!)

I did not call home and tell him our office would close early for the holiday like I normally would. Instead, I walked to the house. The front door was unlocked. Slowly, I tip-toed inside. My breath was shallow so that I wouldn't make any noise. I found the room he was in, his childhood bedroom. The door was cracked slightly. I pushed it open just enough to see two piles of flesh rubbing and jiggling.

I slowly closed the door, left the house as quickly as I could, and walked across the street to a wrecked car company. I asked the owner if I could use his phone. He said yes. I dialed the house, and my husband answered, feigning the most pathetic cough I had ever heard. "Hello."

"Listen, you lying jackass. I walked in on you fucking her," I said.

He gasped, "What are you talking about? You're going crazy."

I told him, "Am I? Look out your window. I'm standing at the garage in front of the house." I saw his bedroom curtains move in the window, and I waved. "Do you see me now? No, I'm not crazy, but I'm done with you! No more lies, and you are out of my life. She can have you."

But he was right. I was crazy. Even after all that, I gave him one last chance. He went back to live with his parents while I strategized a divorce plan. I know how hard it is to let go of a marriage. In my time, it felt like I was the biggest failure. At twenty-three years old, I was still green to the world, and somehow I was approaching a second divorce... was this the story I was meant to live with? What did I do wrong? Could I fix it? Who would want a woman with three daughters? That's what he and his mother would say whenever I thought about leaving.

At the time, I thought it must have been my fault. When faced with this disastrous moment in a marriage or relationship, most women think that. Society puts all of the blame on women. If a man cheats, it's because the woman wasn't good enough. If he hits her, it's because she upset him. If a woman leaves, it's because she's a whore.

None of this is true. Men do what they do, good or bad, because they choose to. My first husband was an abuser, and my second was a cheater. For these reasons, I chose to leave and face the ridicule of my family and my Hispanic culture. I had loved them both and envisioned a forever happiness. Accepting the truth and finding the strength to walk away was painful, but it was still more bearable than staying. It gave my daughters and me the fresh start we deserved.

That's why it was so important for me to tell this story now. Maxi was exactly where I had been. And if you're reading this, you may be or have been too. Listen. The world likes to talk about the resilience of women. Remember, resilience does not mean staying in a bad situation because you're strong. Resilience is not being broken. It's choosing to go on, even when things seem impossible. Resilience is living when circumstances have tried to kill you.

———

A couple of weeks passed, and then I got the call that I expected. Maxi was crying, and she told me she had just gotten served the divorce papers. By then, I had enough information to know that she had a pretty good case against him. Moreover, given that she was legally disabled, he'd even have to pay her support.

"Maxi, ya vez! You see! He has been playing you because he has your number down. So, now what, Maxi? Don't you dare shed another tear for that son of a bitch! Come on, let's sing our pain away." So, for almost a week, we kept singing and healing.

Finally, she got an offer. He would give her ten thousand dollars, and she'd have to move out. What a son of a bitch Sissy Boy turned out to be.

"Can you believe that? He's crazy if he thinks I will settle for ten grand!" Finally, my daughter was angry.

"So, Mija, you need to pay attention to every little thing. He will try tactics that have worked with you in the past—buttering you up, claiming he wants to do this amicably, etc. Think with your head, Mija. He does not deserve an ounce of your heart!"

"But mom, it hurts so much. How could he be this way? I never thought it would come to this. How am I going to deal with my illness? He is the one with insurance, and I haven't worked in at least two years." Her voice broke, and tears started to roll down her cheeks.

"Mija, it will be a hard road, but when you come out of all this, you will look back and be so proud of yourself because you will have grown stronger from this. This man was not going to get out of this unscathed. First, we would have to decline his offer and let his attorney know that we are looking for our attorney. "Wait 'till tomorrow when you have gotten yourself out of all this crying. Cry, scream if you have to, punch a pillow until you get all your stress out. But tomorrow, you call that attorney and give him the news."

I cannot say that all this scared me because it did. However, I knew I had to work hard to keep working with Maxi's blinders. Taking off the blinders would be hard, but she was beginning to peek through. He had fooled her one too many times, and I was sitting on the sidelines pointing this out because it seems you don't want to see when you are in the midst of a divorce. Believe me when I tell you, you have to. You have to face the truth of your situation, or you will pay for it one way or another. So, as you continue reading this, and if you are in crisis, I beg you to seek out anyone that can stand by you. Seek counseling. Seek help. That is what will make you whole again.

CHAPTER 4

MERRY-GO-ROUND

Maxi had not held a job in what I thought had been two years. It turned out she had been unemployed for at least five. Five years living under Egorr's abuse, being torn down board by board like an old house. Now that he was out of the house, the hard work of reconstruction could begin. She started having weekly meetings with a counselor and regular calls with me. My part in this was to listen, be patient, and have those hard conversations.

In one talk, I explained to her that the rest of the family and I were concerned about her wellbeing. We had seen the worst of Sissy Boy and were truly afraid he'd snap under the weight of the divorce. I knew from past experiences that this is when a man or woman could be blinded by emotion. I never forgot that there was still a gun in the house.

One night, she called with such sadness in her voice.

She was quiet, and her voice trembled a little. My heart sank just hearing it because, before this marriage, Maxi was a happy, positive, and confident young lady. She knew what she wanted out of life and was working toward that. Once she met this man, she left all her dreams aside. She began smoking more, claiming that this helped her body pains. The daily battle with pain is something I knew all too well, so I didn't judge her.

"I don't get it, mom," she said through the phone, "How could he have lied to me? He promised he was going to seek help, and he then sent me these divorce papers? He called me and told me he was making sure I was getting the most I could get and for me to just sign the papers. Can you believe that?"

"So, what is he offering this time?" I asked. I expected to hear he'd give her five grand more or something ridiculous like that.

"Well, he proposes that I get thirty grand, no furniture, no car, and no health insurance or spousal support." Her voice broke as if she would start crying soon.

By then, I had made sure Maxi had done diligent work to learn her rights and how much she should expect. Altogether, she should have seen around one-hundred thousand dollars once the house situation was cleared. There was more than enough money in different accounts to make sure my daughter would have a chance at a new beginning.

"So, what do you think now that you know what it should be?" I said calmly.

"I'm torn, mom. I truly believed he cared for me. How could he be so cruel? He knows I'm sick, and I won't be able to work until who knows when. He feels I'm making it up that I'm not sick. It never mattered how many doctors told him I have RA. In his mind, I'm faking it. You know, one time I was having chest pains and fell to the floor because I felt dizzy. He stood above me and laughed as I kept telling him to call 911. He called me a drama queen. I called my own ambulance, and he didn't even come with me. It turned out I needed an urgent heart operation...." What little control she had, she lost, and I listened to her sobs through the phone.

I cried with her—as quietly as I could—because her pain was my pain. "Have you told your counselor all these things, Maxi?"

"Yes, mom," she answered, sniffling.

"And what has he told you?" I asked in a hopeful voice.

"He keeps insisting I get out of this house and move as far away as I can from this man. He says I'm in grave danger and don't want to see it.".

"So, what do you think?" I asked with more hope in my heart.

"I don't know. I mean, he does have a kind heart, and he is a good man, but this behavior began once his parents moved closer to us. We were so happy when they were living in Arkansas. Now, they meddle in everything, and his mom keeps telling me I'm faking it and that I'm lazy. So I think that's what's caused him to become like that." I paused and thought carefully for maybe a little too long. "Mom? Are you still there?"

"So, what are you thinking about the divorce offer?" I asked. I pushed her harder to see that what he was offering her as a resolution to their divorce was terrible.

"I don't know. Maybe I should go ahead and take it. He told me if I did that, we could just make it seem as if we are divorcing and that he'd take care of me, but he did not want his parents to know he was going to do that." My heart seized. Typical. Narcissistic folks trying to screw a good-hearted woman. They had a sizable bank account, and the house she was staying in was fully paid for. I was not going to let her eat that fat lie.

"Maxi, you better not sign those documents. Do you truly believe him? After all of what you are telling me he has done to you and the family has done, you are telling me that you are just going to roll over? So, why do all this drama and why stay in that house? Let me go for you if that's the decision you are taking because you won't be able to cover any medical or housing with that amount. The moment you sign those documents, you will have to leave that house. Did not you read that part?"

She had sent me the offer through PDF, and I was reading it fervently. I heard her say under her breath, "That son of a bitch."

The attorney that Sissy Boy had suggested Maxi get was not doing much work to help her with this divorce. The office would forget to send her documents or claim they did not receive documents. I was on top of things trying to make sure that she had that support because I knew how difficult it was to navigate a divorce while my health was in shambles. My last husband had decided that he wanted out of our marriage for the exact same reasons this man was getting out. "For better and for worse. In sickness and in health." means nothing to this kind of scum. I had loved my ex like no one else. Unfortunately, during our fourth year of blissful marriage, I began to exhibit signs of serious health issues. Maxi kept telling me that she was not as sick as I had been because at least she was not in a wheelchair. I had to be in a wheelchair and had to depend on him to help me when I went anywhere. The look that Sissy Boy had when he left Maxi was a look I knew all too well. Maxi was still in partial denial. I was not going to let her get screwed over like I did. I'm sure Sissy Boy was counting on her not being well enough mentally to navigate this divorce, but just like I had told him, I was, and I was not about to leave her alone. Maxi kept looking at the divorce offer, and I could tell she was getting angrier as she read on.

"Look at page three. Do you see Maxi? He states that he won't pay for any health insurance or anything that has to do with your 'addiction.' If you are not mad about this, I am. What is your attorney doing?"

"He keeps saying I won't be able to get half of what I want." She said with clear frustration in her voice.

"I don't understand why he is saying that, Maxi. Have you read the information I sent you about the rights you have? Also, the one about spousal abuse: what it is and what it is not? The fact that he did everything he did to you and that you have people who are willing to step up and give a deposition about it, well, you may need to change this attorney. I have my doubts he is working for your best interest. Ask him all those questions. It's your right to make sure your attorney gets a clear picture and gets the most he can for you." At that point, I told Maxi I would write an email for her with all of the questions she should ask. She would not be alone, and she would not be left with nothing.

She agreed, and I typed it then and there. She looked at the email and hit send immediately. When she spoke, she sounded a little bit more upbeat but still sad. So, like every other night, I invited her to get online and sing karaoke with me. The songs she had been singing up until that day were sad songs of lost love. Today, for the first time, she sang a song about fighting back. I forget the song's name, but I knew at that precise moment that Maxi was starting to get angry. That's the sign I had been waiting for.

You can probably relate to this type of drama. What divorce exists without all the drama? (If there was no drama, there probably wouldn't be a divorce!) You go round and round but never really get anywhere, and after a while, you're stuck wondering if you will ever get off that merry-go-round. I'm here to tell you that you need to keep going. There will be a better tomorrow.

You may not have that mother, sister, or friend. That is unfair but OK. You don't have to judge yourself, and you still don't have to be alone. It just means it's time to seek out help, find a new community of people who can look from the outside, and stop the cycle. Joining a church group or even a Facebook group for women that are going through divorce are a couple of easy options.

Going through a divorce or any crisis in life alone is very hard on you. I know. I had to do it because I couldn't truly count on family or friends to be there for me. As a survivor of child abuse and later of spousal abuse, I learned to isolate myself. It was a form of self-preservation. Well, eventually, you will have to face the fact that it just doesn't work well enough for anyone. So, slowing down the merry-go-round is the only way, and it may take all-hands-on-deck.

Take time for yourself. Go on long walks. Get back to things that you enjoy. In other words, it's time to get off the ride. I knew it was time to push my Maxi off the merry-go-round one way or another. It's not something I was looking forward to, but, as a mama bear, I had to save her.

Chapter 5

Stop the Merry-Go-Round

I could not help but think how that one incident had likely caused this generational trauma. From reading so many psychology studies, I learned that family trauma was a generational thing. I laid there till morning broke, thinking about my mother and what had caused her to be the abusive parent she had been.

A child, a horse, and a stick. That's how all this family trauma started. As most mothers do, I wondered what I had done to leave my girl vulnerable to this abuse. I had doted on my girls up until I became ill. Even then, I was always cuddling and making sure they knew I loved them. Had I overdone it? Had I inadvertently done things that caused her to accept abuse?

Well, if I had, I had to undo it. I had first to find out what I had done wrong to her and ask for forgiveness—something my mother would have never done. I would have to have the conversation about how I had to forgive my mother by first understanding her and then by allowing all that anger to dissipate. It would be more of those hard conversations, but they had to happen. I wondered if maybe the fact that I had stayed away from my mother to save my girls from her abuse had caused this man to easily pull her from me. Maybe, just maybe, not having that relationship with my own mother taught my girls that that's the way it should be. I was eager to hear the phone ring.

The day went by ever so slowly. I wanted to know if the attorney had responded or not. The email I had put together for her would cause her attorney to either step it up or leave her high and dry. I had talked to Maxi about all those possibilities and had prepared her for the future. Finally, the phone rang, and Maxi was in good spirits. She sounded well.

"Hey, mom! So, before you ask, I have not heard from the attorney, but Sissy Boy called to tell me he thinks he should put in the divorce that he will cover my medical for at least a year. He just did it, I guess, because he feels guilty. I told you, mom, he's still a good person. It's his parents that are behind all this." She said.

Here we go again, I thought. "Hey, Mija, are those cameras still working? You know, the ones that are outside where you like to sit, smoke, and talk to me?" Silence. Then it all came out hurling. Anger.

"Damnit! Damnit, and fuck him! Those cameras are

working, and he's probably been watching and listening to everything we talk about. That piece of shit! Gotta go, mom. I need to take care of those cameras." Click. Silence.

For a split second, when I had helped him convince Maxi to separate, I had my doubts that I was doing right by her. After this call, all doubt was gone. No longer did I feel that I was meddling too much. I had to save my girl from this monster. What else did I not know? What else were he and his parents capable of? According to Maxi and Sissy Boy, his parents had amassed a fortune somehow. I wondered about it until, finally, my phone rang again.

"Maxi, are you ok? Is everything ok?" I asked.

"Yes. I turned off all the cameras, and if he comes into the house in the next thirty minutes demanding I turn them back on, I will call the cops on him." Good, I thought.

"Since I have you on the phone now, I want you to hear your grandma's story. I've been doing a whole lot of thinking, and I've come to the realization that maybe, just maybe, the reason he so easily manipulated you is because that's what you saw growing up. You saw a mother who had no connection to her own mother or very little connection to her siblings. So, I want you to hear what I have to say. Maybe you can put things into perspective, and we can begin changing this separation that's been built in our family." I said.

"He has been manipulating me by hearing and seeing everything I do! Why did I not even think that that's what he was doing?" She said, nearly yelling. "I've been such an idiot!"

Maxi was beginning to see what he was. I knew it was another hit to her heart, but I was hoping that she would reach this point. It's the first crucial step toward freedom because you have to see the lies you've believed so you can reject them. It feels embarrassing and upsetting, but this is why having support can be so beneficial. When your mind wants to beat you up for being so stupid, you have people to hold onto the other side of reality and remind you that you just believed too much in goodness. It's not dumb to hope your partner can change. Now it was time for her to learn the real story as to why I was able to move on from my life crisis. It was time to be vulnerable again.

"Do you remember how mean and grouchy your grandma was? Abusive to the teeth. Well, all my life, I've wondered why she was like that. Something inside me told me that there had to be a trigger that made her that way."

When I was pursuing my psychology degree, I came across a section about trauma. So I wondered for years if maybe my mom had experienced some kind of trauma that was never dealt with. In her time, the cart and horses era, there was no listening to children. Children were seen, not heard. The number of times I heard that from my elders was more than enough to realize that they never ever talked about any kind of trauma. They just boxed it up and put it away in a red TNT box.

So, when my brother got married a few years back, I found my answer. One of my uncles came to me and told me that I needed to be more understanding toward my mother. I told him that he knew nothing about what had happened to me. I was still very hurt about the physical, sexual, and mental abuse in my childhood. I thought I would never ever be able to forgive her, and I carried that anger for most of my life. It was dragging me down without me knowing. I wondered, sometimes, if that was the reason I became sickly. There is evidence that abuse does that to a person, but I never followed that thought very long.

Empathy. Sometimes it hits you when you least expect it. This was one of those moments when life had dealt me an empathy sandwich of sorts. For years I had been mad at my mom for not being there for me, but my uncle was about to give me one of those life lessons you never forget.

My uncle told me the most unusual story. My mother was a typical child. She grew up on a farm and had many wonderful memories that she used to talk about. Most of them involved doing what children do, you know, play pranks on each other. As kids, they'd goof around by riding the animals. Sometimes she'd grab a stick and poke pigs or any other animal in the ass. She thought it was so funny to see pigs, goats, or any other animal react as they did. Then my uncle gave me another piece of the puzzle.

One day, my dad and my mother were getting ready to go into town. In those days, it was a full-day affair. They had to get the cart attached to the horse and make sure the horse had good horseshoes on and all that. My uncle, who was old enough at the time, placed the horse and cart right in front of the door of the house to make it easier to put things in. My family sold things like corn and farm food like that. He walked away to begin loading, so he didn't see everything, but in a blink of an eye, the horse jumped on its hind legs, and right at the same time, my grandma walked outside.

The horse knocked her over with its front legs. Before anyone could reach her, the horse came down right on her stomach. They pulled her from under the horse, and there standing behind the horse with a stick in her hand, was my mom. No one was sure if she poked its ass, but that's what it looked like. My uncle suggested that mom had developed some mental issues because of that day.

Maxi couldn't believe it when I told her this. She wanted to tell her sisters right then!

"Mija, hold on to your horses," I joked, "It took me a while before I could put things into perspective. Imagine being that age and causing that kind of accident. Truly imagine it, Maxi. You know, your grandma called me one day and, for the first time, talked about her mother and told me how your oldest sister looks so much like her mom. She told me that she wished her mom would have never died of that disease. So, in order to make things make sense, your grandma was told that her mother had died from a made-up disease, or she made that up to cope with that type of trauma.

It's truly a really sad story, Maxi. Imagine growing up with no mother as a girl. She lacked the love of a mother, so she did not know how to show love. The worst part of it all is that my grandpa became an alcoholic for years after that incident. He, from what I've gathered, ignored your grandma. He'd leave her with his brothers or sisters, and she'd have to earn her keep by working as their maid. She mentioned a few times how they'd beat the shit out of her if she did anything wrong."

Despite everything my mom had put me through, I couldn't help feeling sad about her life. What I went through was a reflection of her experience. Once again, hurt people hurt people. Part of maturing and healing is learning that generational pain hurts everyone. My mom was a victim too. This doesn't excuse the things she did, but it helps me understand her. I could have turned out more like her, but I decided to break the cycle of pain.

Learning to be empathetic and not judgmental of others' lives is key to becoming a whole person yourself. It's easy to point the finger at someone and judge them. It's hard to sit and listen to hard life truths. I can't say that I repaired the relationship with my mother, but I was able to understand her. To feel her pain as if it was my own because it was in so many ways my own. Now it was Maxi's.

"So, in the last few years I spent away from everyone, I was able to make peace with all the abuse," I said to

Maxi. "I forgave your grandma the day she was dying. She could not speak or anything, and mind you, I had to be there via Skype, but I was there. It was the hardest thing I've had to do to say, 'I forgive you, mother. I forgive all the times you beat me until I was numb from all the beatings. I forgive all the horrible names you called me. Most of all, I forgive the fact that you allowed your oldest son to sexually use me as his woman for years. I forgive you.'" I was crying by that point. I heard Maxi sniffling on the other end too.

"What do you mean she allowed your brother to sexually abuse you. What else has happened to you, mom?" I had said too much. However, it was time, time to let my girls know how much I had worked toward making sure no one abused them and why.

"Maxi, if I can forgive her, maybe it's time for you to tell me in and tell me what you are holding onto. There's something in your childhood that maybe you are holding onto and feel that I wronged you for." Silence.

There was a brief interruption as Sissy Boy arrived at their house (again, as if on cue), demanding she turned the cameras back on. He told her it was so he could keep her safe, but I knew that it was so he could keep tabs on her when she was coming and going. She didn't budge, and he left. We talked about that and then came back to my question.

"It's funny that you are asking me about this," Maxi said. "You know the years you were sick and bedridden and all that. I was in middle school. Well, I did have a whole lot of anger against you for not being able to do things with us. I mean, you went from being an all-out mother that was always there for us to be sick and in bed. Now, I get it. It's almost as if God did this to me by giving me this RA thing as punishment. I hated you for not coming to some of my events. I was so selfish back then. Now, I think I'm finally putting things into perspective. Especially given that you had no control over that disease." She sighed.

This was a big revelation. Not necessarily because I didn't know (I did). It was important to understand the "merry-go-round" of life. The things that happen to us are sometimes passed down from our parents and previous generations until we learn to heal the open wound. I resented my mom until she died for the abuse she inflicted on me, but she was abused first. Maxi held onto resentment toward me for not being well enough to care for her the way she needed, and here she was experiencing a similar condition. Lessons repeat until they are learned, and when we don't learn, life becomes this cycle.

"We need to let go of those things," I said. "Anger and resentment do nothing to us but to bring us down. Do you truly think I would do things on purpose to hurt you? That is what's wrong with us. We need to open up those lines of communication and make sure we ask for clarification. I don't think most people set out to do harm to anyone else. I mean, not the good ones. Most people want to love and be loved. Simple as that."

Maxi nodded. She seemed to be working it out, but I

think she understood. I told her to ask her counselor to give her information on generational trauma. If you're reading this book, I invite you to look it up as well. Read about how sometimes behaviors jump from generation to generation. I think that's what has happened to us. And to think so much suffering came from a child, a horse, and a fucking stick!

CHAPTER 6

FIND YOUR LIFE VEST

The ringing of the cell phone woke me up. I looked at the clock, and it was close to seven at night. It was Maxi. Good thing I had slept as much as I had. She sounded anxious, angry, and confused. "That son-of-a-bitch told me he's no longer my attorney. Mom, I think your email was too harsh! He does not want me as his client!" she said, panicking.

I said to her, "OK, Maxi, everything will be alright. I think this might be for the best. I mean, what was he doing on your behalf? Just calm down. Let me call you back because I just woke up. Don't go spinning out of control!" So with that, I hung up.

Here we go again, I thought, another fire to be put out. This one was good, though. I truly believed that this so-called attorney Maxi had was somehow conspiring with Sissy Boy, her soon-to-be ex. COVID was complicating things, but I knew we would get through things one way or another.

I fixed myself some food—eggs, chorizo, and a coffee—and ate quickly so I could call Maxi back right away. Unfortunately, she was crying again when she picked up. I thought she was having some form of an anxiety attack.

"How am I going to get another attorney? I'm calling everyone I can call, and they are all telling me no. It's almost as if I'm doomed. Then Egorr called and was yelling at me. He said that no one could work with me because I was hard to deal with. He's blaming me for the whole thing, and it's your fault, mom. I should not have listened to you."

My heart sank, and I felt physically weak for a moment. "Mija, calm down. I've already talked to a couple of attorneys who have dealt with this type of situation. Both have agreed to hear us out." I slowly calmed her down by talking her threw some breathing and helping her bring the situation back down to size.

Breathing. It's easy. We don't think about it, so we forget it is one of the most effective tools to calm ourselves. In the classroom, I taught my students to calm down by using a breathing technique. In moments of intense pressure, we can spiral out of control—especially when the stakes are high, there's lots of emotion, and we don't want to show our weakness. Suppose you find yourself spiraling out of control. In that case, I highly recommend you try this breathing technique known as the "anchoring heart" technique. Suppose you tend to have anxiety or high levels of stress in your life. In that case, it can become a powerful addition to your personal toolbox. It goes like this:

Step 1: Place one or both hands tenderly over your heart. Relax your shoulders, face, and jaw. Take deep, slow breaths.

Step 2: Allow yourself to feel whatever it is you are feeling. Even if it's just for a short few seconds.

Step 3: Make sure you take a few minutes to sense your being. You know, that place inside of you where you carry your distress. Keep breathing until you begin feeling calm again.

After I had Maxi use the anchoring heart technique, we hung up, and she called both attorney's and both agreed to see her. Since I had been expecting this, I had already spoken with two attorneys who both specialized in dealing with scumbags like Sissy Boy. She was excited about it all. She liked the bigger firm better because they had the funds to work through the case, and what they told her was that she was entitled to half of what they had accumulated and that she would likely win the case if they went to court. Especially given the abuse. Yes, they assured her that what she had gone through was spousal abuse.

She apologized for blaming me and acknowledged that

she was not herself. That is an important step in recovering from trauma and abuse. Unfortunately, you sometimes behave erratically and lash out at people who are trying to help because your identity and nervous systems are so derailed.

The truth was if anyone was going to understand exactly what she was going through, it was me. I figured if this attorney dropped her was ill-prepared to take on Sissy Boy and his family, then he'd jump ship. The sooner that happened, the better for us. That way, we could get a better attorney that's better equipped.

"We will figure it all out, Mija. I'm here for you." I said.

She sighed. "Mom, how did you get so good at things like this. I mean, the number of times I've seen you solve things and still keep your cool. I don't think I would have been able to do it like you have. I don't think I'm as strong as you are."

"Well, I have God on my side. Always have. Ever since I can remember, I've been aware of him. I have to tell you about how I met up with him and how he's the reason I've been able to survive what I have. Have I told about the tent that would come to our neighborhood every summer?" I asked.

"No. What tent? Here we go, another one of your famous stories."

When I was maybe three or four years old, I woke up to the noise of hammering and voices right outside our house. There was a huge empty circular lot in front of my mother's house. It has since been turned into a park, but for years that lot sat there empty because no matter what the city put there, the older kids would destroy it. The noises woke all of us up. There were all these white teenagers in our Hispanic neighborhood. I had no idea why these teens would literally risk their lives in our neighborhood.

The commotion woke people up and down the street too. Our neighbors got together, wondering what these white teens were doing. Then several of them began approaching all the houses. They were passing out some pamphlets that had stuff written in both English and Spanish. I heard my mom talking to the neighbor about it. They were going to start a sort of bible summer camp here in our neighborhood. So the tent was for that. The neighbors were laughing and ridiculing the poor teens. No one would send their kids to a FREE summer bible camp, they claimed. Anyway, my mom saw it as an opportunity to get rid of at least three or four of her kids.

Soon enough, the neighborhood ladies were all for it. So early the next morning, several of my brothers and sisters got cleaned up and were sent to the church tent. I was not old enough to go that first year when the tent came. I remember going to the porch to watch them. It looked like a fun place but living in a poor neighborhood and placing a tent in the middle of it, well, something like that would certainly bring the hood kids out. That evening, several hooligans from the neighborhood had a party under the tent. They decided to get high, and they tore up the tent. The next morning these teens still had bible study under a torn tent. That evening, they took down the tent, and from that point forward, they'd come back and set up the tent at around five in the morning, and they'd take down the tent by like three or four in the afternoon. Can you imagine the amount of conviction they had to bring God into our lives? I'm sure they knew many of us needed God.

I admired them. The work ethic and the drive they had. I knew about church and the bible, but I really was still too young to understand it all. The following year, I was ever so ready to go to the tent. The best part of it was that on Friday, they would give us "raspas" (ice slushies), and we could choose whichever flavor we wanted. You can imagine why most kids went to the bible studies. That was something we rarely, if ever, got to experience as kids, and here we were eating slushies for free. It was there that I learned about Jesus and the whole bible thing. I know it's not for everyone, and I learned to respect that, but I count myself as one of the very lucky ones to have listened.

"Maxi," I said, "in life, we have to find what I consider is our life vest or life jacket. We have to believe in something, so we don't drown in sorrow and despair. For me, it has been God. I believe in God and his promise of everlasting love in the afterlife. That hope is exactly what I needed to be able to survive all the trials and tribulations life has thrown in my direction."

I often wonder about people that don't believe in

God. I wonder what it is that drives them and what it is that fills the sorrows in their life because, believe me, life can bring you many sorrows, and if you have nothing that can pull you up from that, you could easily drown in them. However, I've met people that don't believe in God, and they are good people. In fact, through my travels, I met many teachers, principals, and others who refused to believe there was such a thing as God. I have learned to respect those differences. They have a different belief system that does the exact same thing my belief system does. Help us survive life and appreciate the love for one another.

For me, God has always been my life jacket, the only way I know to survive life's tribulations. I've never pushed my girls to believe in God or anything like that. I allowed them to make their own decisions as far as that goes. In fact, I pulled away from religion because I truly don't agree with many of the things they push on people, but I have not pulled away from believing in God. Otherwise, for me, life would have been catastrophic. What has always helped me stand strong was knowing God is by my side no matter what.

I learned so many things in that little tent church. They did not push any type of religious denomination on us. They did not try to convert us into this or that. They simply told us about a man named Jesus Christ who died on the cross for us. They would divide us up into groups, and we would do little activities like create a cross from lollipop sticks and then decorate it with things they brought, like glitter. Year after year, they kept coming back, and year after year, I'd be one of the first to show up. These individuals expected nothing from us but gave us hope.

Remembering the love and compassion in their eyes and how nice they were to every single child brings tears to my eyes to this day. They were risking everything. The neighborhood we lived in puts any tough "hood" in the USA to shame. Still, these white teens show up. I can't tell you how many times we'd see shootings and dead bodies in that park. How many times we'd seen young girls having sex in that park. Cars would come by and park there at night, and they'd either be dealing drugs, having sex, or killing someone. These young people didn't care. Whoever that church was, they were true angels in disguise.

There's one other thing that came out of that little church tent. Songs. I know in my heart of hearts that's when I fell in love with singing. I used to think that it was my mom's singing and that I just wanted to sing as well as she sang. It was not until after she died that I realized that my love of singing was the one thing deep inside me that helped me cope with everything that was happening around me.

That's when I truly was touched by God, at least in my heart. He gave me that love for singing as a gift. The little songs we sang, I still remember to this day. I began singing, This little light of mine, I'm gonna let it shine! This little light of mine, I'm gonna let it shine... There was one that says, Jesus loves me, yes I know, for the bible tells me so. A gift I will die with.

You need to find your life jacket. I know you have one in you. Put it on and never ever take it off. Hug it when you feel lost or when you feel as if life is too hard to handle. Everyone around the world comes across days like that. Days that you will feel like dying or just giving up. Those days you hug your jacket, and you reach out to your loved ones. That group of people won't judge you or try to manipulate you. Always have those kinds of friends or family around. Always.

I'm encouraging this for you because, if I'm honest, I haven't always had this type of community or been good at forming one. Truth be told, I've gotten so good at this life-jacket life, holding onto what I can keep close, that I rarely reach out to anyone. I just hate giving others my burdens, which is what many women feel when they start to realize they have a problem.

In my case, the people around me expressed a clear disregard for my problems, so I sheltered myself and learned to make it on my own. This is not the easier or better way all of the time. It has led me to deal with things alone for a lot longer than I needed to. Vulnerability is hard and takes courage. It was because of my Maxi I was learning to be vulnerable. I had to so she could have a model and learn as well. In doing so, we would help heal each other, and I knew it.

"You know how I know you so well?" I said. "It's because you are taking a similar path in life to the one I did. You have been taken advantage of by people who undervalue your kindness. That happens to me too. However, I still want to believe that through trials, we find people who are true friends. True family members.

I believe that as we get older, we get better at not needing such a big group. It's just part of preparing ourselves to start the next chapters in our old lives. That's losing those that we love. So, as a mom, and even if you don't want to hear it, we are not here forever. I'm getting old, and well, sooner or later, life will be gone from me. I need to make sure you become a strong woman so you can take on life. You hate when I say things like that, but I'm no longer a young sexy chicken. " I paused to listen.

I heard nothing on the other side of the phone. "Maxi, are you there?"

"Yes, mom. I was just listening to you and lost in thought. I was wondering who my team of friends and family would be. I know you are, but I'm not quite sure about my sisters. I mean, I feel so judged by them. Instead of just listening to me and maybe giving me a hug or two, they start telling me how I need to do this or that. You know. It just feels like they are judging me harshly," she said.

This is why many of us have deep-seated unresolved trauma. Shame, judgment, fear, and our own egos.

"Maxi, this is something we need to work out. I don't want you to think that way. Do you want to know why you are thinking that way? It's because you've been in a situation in which a man has been putting you down constantly, and you now believe that everyone is judging you. Your sisters can be judgy at times, I know, but think about what they are saying and why they are saying it. Could it be that they want to help you but don't know what to say?"

Maxi was judging them from her feelings. When we're in a situation where people don't give us the support we think we need, it can feel like we're being scrutinized because we're already sensitive. It's like when a child falls and scrapes their knee. Sometimes they don't want the alcohol wipe. They just want the Band-Aid and the kiss to feel better. What we have to remember is that sometimes the people around us genuinely want to help but may not realize that you are seeking comfort, not advice. When they jump to trying to solve your problem by telling you what to do, try to remember that they think their helping. You don't have to take it. You can tell them you feel judged, but remember that there's another side to the coin.

"When you talk to them, are you judging them?" I asked.

"I mean, sometimes if they are doing something stupid," she said, giggling.

"What do you mean by doing something stupid?" I really wanted to see if she could see it from the other side.

"Well, you know, like maybe dating someone who is not right for them or is cheating on them? I'd definitely tell them, but sometimes they get mad at me for telling them, so it's a no-win situation as far as I can see."

"How would you tell them about a cheating boyfriend?"

"I don't know. I'd be like, 'Hey, he's cheating on you. You need to leave him!'" she laughed.

"Exactly my point! Do you see how you said it? Before you decide that your sisters are being mean to you, think about the intentions in their words. Are they saying those things to you because they don't know how else to help you or because they feel judged by you? You see?" I asked, trying to see if she got my messed-up message.

"Yes, mom. I get it. I just have my doubts," she said in a somber way.

"If you don't start trying to make sure you have family around you to help you when you need help, you will be out at sea with no one to talk to. That's when people get crazy thoughts in their heads." I got to learn about all that in Korea. The number of teens who commit suicide out there is incredible. It comes from feeling isolated during vulnerable moments and being told to push our feelings down. Now it's happening here in the United States and all because we don't help each other out. The truth is, we need each other.

This is the part of the story where I have to point out something obvious. Maxi had slowly fallen prey to a narcissist who had pushed all her family and friends away from her. Leaving her alone and vulnerable to his abuse. It was like being in the water with a shark. Sometimes a life jacket isn't enough. You need to be in a lifeboat with at least five or six other people to help you. I know that it's hard to see ourselves as vulnerable, but we are all vulnerable if we aren't in a boat and wearing our life jackets.

I pointed out to Maxi that she had two sisters, a cousin, and an aunt and uncle who loved her dearly. I pointed out her friends as well because they were still around and would no doubt still be there if she ever reached out.

Whatever is happening in your life, I'm sure you will try to either reach out to those that love you, or you will begin working on having more friends around. It's time for you to start looking at your future and start healing. You have so much to look forward to. You have your whole life ahead of you. Sick or not, someone is out there that will love you as dearly as I love my daughters.

I mean, look at me, how many times was I told that no one would want me for being dark, or for having kids, or for being sickly, or whatever other crappy reason they people could make up. People that tell you things like that are the type of folks you need to kick out or let them know they are crossing a line. You have every God-given right to decide who will be in your boat. We all do.

Chapter 7

Emerge

The morning came, and I woke up to Opal barking. I took some time to get out of bed, and I thought the worst of the divorce was over, but boy, was I wrong! Sissy Boy had frozen the bank accounts, locking Maxi out. Any funds that she had access to were no longer available to her—a typical narcissist tactic. He wanted to make her sign by not allowing her any access to the funds. Apparently, his attorney was playing dirty as well.

This unscrupulous attorney had called my girl early that morning, yelling at her, demanding she sign the divorce. She said he had told her there was no way she would get an attorney to work with her because the attorneys in the area would know she was an addict, as stated by Sissy Boy. These two men figured if they cut Maxi off financially, she'd become desperate enough to accept whatever they wanted.

Unknown to either one of them, my brother Roland

had stepped in and funded the initial attorney's fees of Maxi's new attorney. After Sissy Boy's attorney finished yelling at my daughter, my daughter calmly explained to him that he needed to contact her attorney. He had all of the information and would be dealing with the case from that point forward. That day, she called me victorious. She said her phone had been going off with text messages from Sissy Boy claiming that she probably stole some of his money and that he was going to figure out how she was able to secure an attorney.

She could not wait to respond to him, but she first called me and asked me, "What should I do, mom? Should I respond?" I could hear the delight and excitement in her voice. She finally had Sissy Boy sweating bullets because a narcissist like Sissy Boy hates to lose control over people.

I immediately jumped in my car and headed out there. I must have broken, I don't know how many speed limits, but I was afraid he'd get so upset that he'd try getting back in the house. My brother and I had ensured she had established contacts with the neighbors and that the neighbors knew she was in imminent danger. So, I got there right in time. As I got there, I saw his car pulling up behind me. He was livid, but the gun was in the house, and he did not have access to it until he decided he had to have it.

We were on the phone with Maxi's attorney, and he was on the phone with Sissy Boy's attorney. Sissy Boy's attorney was playing "dumb," claiming he was not aware of a gun and was not able to reach his client. Anyway, long story short, I walked into the house first. I knew he feared me, so I told him he was not allowed to go in until Maxi decided it was OK. I closed the door and locked it behind me. He rang the doorbell several times, and we waited to hear from the attorney. Finally, Maxi's attorney called. "You have to allow him in the house. The other attorney you had never filed the protective order. I will call the police department, but they won't be able to do a thing. They will be on stand-by." With that, he hung up and did his thing.

Sissy Boy was fuming, but I was not going to let him get close to Maxi. He tried to play it cool. Oh, I just came for more of my personal things, and I want to open the safe to get my passport. Maxi was ready, "Well, I thought you had lost the keys to the safe when I had asked for my passport and my jewelry. Did you find the keys?" she said in a very soft and calm voice. I could sense she still feared him. His mother was outside in the car waiting on him. Typical Sissy Boy behavior. They were now claiming that the house was not under Sissy Boy's name but rather his parents' name. Typical switcheroo. We had him on recordings saying it was his house, but they had changed everything to his parents' name a couple of years ago. Maxi had no idea.

He went to a drawer and pulled it out. On the back of the drawer, the "lost" key to the safe was taped to it. Maxi had told me she had looked everywhere and this weird behavior of taping a key in that form was a sign that this man was used to "hiding" things. So, he opened the safe. Pulled the gun and brandished it in our direction. I could see there were no bullets in it. I stepped forward, and he recoiled. He immediately put it down and said he was taking it with him. He was unaware that Maxi had started recording everything that was happening with her cell phone. He said, "I need this gun with me. It's a really good gun, and I need to practice shooting it. You know, so I can hit my mark if I ever need to use it." He said with a smirk on his face. Maxi did not flinch.

"Oh wow, yeah, you need that because your other gun is worthless," I said in a taunting voice as I looked at his crotch area. He pushed the gun into the belt of his pants.

"He thinks he's a man!" I said, mocking him. "Look at him. How ridiculous can he be?"

"You fucking bitch! Your nothing but a feminazi!" He yelled at me. I had decided at that moment that I was going to be proud of the title he had given me instead of insulted.

He looked at Maxi. "I hate your mother." Then he looked at me. "Maxi is a user, you know. She's a lying bitch like you!"

Maxi chimed in, "I'm no longer believing anything you tell me, Egorr. From this point forward, if you have something to say to me, you do it through my new attorney." As Maxi was yelling at him, he was walking backward, and at that precise moment, I saw my girl get her power back from him.

"You fucking pair of crazy feminazis!" He yelled as he

began walking toward the door. He had not even grabbed any of his supposed personal items. All he wanted was to somehow get at Maxi so he could intimidate her.

This is something that happens when a marriage has become too toxic. Again I say that once a woman begins to be assertive and raises her voice, society will treat her as a crazy woman. Men, on the other hand, are assertive. It's a played-out double-standard. If you feel shame for having to stand up for yourself, don't. Empower the one person they have been victimizing. Stand by her until she can be as bold as my Maxi was learning to be. It's alright to get crazy if all you are getting is crazy. Just make sure you don't lose yourself in those moments. Come out victorious and assertive. Don't allow anyone to shame you for being assertive and standing up to a bully like this one.

"Come on now, get out of here!" I told him. "If you have nothing else to do here, let me tell you that from this point forward, I'm going to be staying here. Oh, and I'm sure you will be receiving a protective order in the next few days. Oh, and I know about the rapes in college and the rape of that young girl in that apartment complex you lived in. You are what's called a serial rapist, and believe me, you, the authorities of Texas will be informed of your past activities!" I said with conviction. He looked at Maxi and then at me, "Oh, and don't try to deny it. We have your latest victim's information, so you better be watching for cops closing in on you," I lied.

"Maxi, I can't believe you told her! You were not supposed to tell anyone. Oh, it's all a lie." He was caught once again. I was so disgusted by this piece of scum. I walked right behind him. So close he'd look back with worried eyes. "Didn't your attorney say he was sending the cops over, Maxi?" I asked loudly so that the mother could hear.

"Ah, yes. They should be here soon enough." He nearly tripped as he made it into the car.

At that precise moment, his mother opened her window. "I don't want you in my house, you nigger," she said to me with broken English.

I hoped so badly she would get out of the car and come up to me. I'd wanted to give her a piece of my mind for years. I had never seen this woman since the wedding. That day, the woman sat in the front row, but while the vows were being said, she turned her chair to give her back to the ceremony. Every person at the wedding was wondering who she was. Her husband, Egorr's father, tried to be polite, but I pulled them to one side and told both of them, "I don't know where you got educated, but what you did on this day was childish and unacceptable."

The woman said nothing. Sissy Boy's father apologized on her behalf and said they'd stay for dinner but nothing else. The whole time we were eating, she was throwing darts from her eyes as she looked at Maxi. Later on, we found out that they were very upset because my daughter was dark like me. They were further upset because several of her male friends were gay, and one of them decided to sing for them. He had a beautiful voice, and everyone stood up and clapped for the couple. It was an amazing wedding. This was the second time I would ever see that woman.

I have to say something about us women. For centuries we have birthed sons and taught them to be "macho" or "manly." What does that even mean? Usually insensitive, aggressive indulgent, unapologetic, and egoistic. This is not a diss on masculinity, but I am calling out the tendencies I see over and over in men who follow this "be a man" creed. Then we taught our daughters to tend to them as if they were kings. Ladies, it's high time to rethink how we raise our boys. If you have both daughters and sons, think about how you treat them. Are you allowing your daughters to be assertive, or do you shut them down? Are you raising future narcissistic men? I know many women who are now divorced and wish they would have raised their sons differently. Women today aren't willing to put up with this kind of behavior. We need to rethink the way we are raising our sons so they too can be successful in marriage and in life. Fathers need to do the same. Unfortunately, it was too late for Egorr to learn those lessons. It was clear to me that this fruit had fallen very close to the tree, and it was rotting.

We watched the car drive off, and right at that moment, a police car turned into the street. They stopped and asked if we were OK, and we said we were. It brought us great joy to see that he had surely pooped in his pants when he saw the cops pass by him. The attorney called and let us know that he had requested a police officer check on us. We told him that Sissy Boy had taken the gun. He told us that would only be worse for Sissy Boy's case as he would file an urgent order in court regarding the gun.

We went inside and locked the door. I hugged Maxi. I was so proud of her! That's how you stand up to jerks like Sissy Boy. No matter how much trembling you feel inside, you don't let a jerk like him know it. The more you show them fear, the more they will take control over you. When you stand up for yourself and hold your ground, they lose control. This is why it's so important to have connections with other people. When it's just you alone, you're not a threat. When you have friends who have your back, well, it's much harder for them to manipulate. This is why Sissy Boy was so frustrated. This is why I know you, too, can be successful at becoming a feminazi, a warrior, a survivor.

I decided Maxi would not be alone at the house anymore. I was going to stay with her, and when I couldn't, my brother Roland and his wife Sonia would be there. Roland and Sonia had been so supportive in all this. They wanted to get back to having a strong and healthy relationship like we had before my daughter met her husband. Sissy Boy told so many lies to all of us, and we were all uncovering the truth now. When it came to my brother, Sissy Boy called him and said Maxi no longer wanted to have any kind of relationship with him because he was not good for her mental wellbeing. Sissy Boy said that once she was better, she would reach out to him. My brother, being the kind, gentle giant he is, did not push the matter. He accepted Sissy Boy's explanation. All of them did, and of course, I was away from the country, so I had no idea this was going on. All I knew was that it was getting harder and harder to get a hold of anyone in my family.

Maxi was outside smoking, and I went out there as well. "I sure wish you would quit smoking, Mija. Those things kill you, you know." I said.

"I know, mom. I'm going to cut back and then quit once this divorce is done with," she said, but there was no conviction in her voice. "He really didn't expect me to be strong again. Even though I was scared, it did feel good to see him afraid of us. I get it now. Don't show men like him any fear. That's what makes them feel powerful."

"Now, Maxi, you never ever let a man belittle you, ever. You make sure you let them know you are not to be treated that way. Don't let any man or even a woman get away with any little thing, even if they tell you things like 'I was just playing' or 'you took it wrong.' You make sure you tell them that you won't put up with any name-calling or any kind of behavior that makes you feel uncomfortable."

I will never understand how a mother would raise her son to behave this way. I felt sorry for Sissy Boy. I wondered what happened in that house to make him how he was. I also knew that it was not my girl's fault. It was his messed-up upbringing. But he was an adult, and he could have gotten the proper help he needed. Instead, he hurt others with his venom. I knew he came from a family that fears counseling because they fear facing the ugly truth about themselves.

"Next time, Maxi, you will take your time to get to know the man AND the family. Pay close attention to their behavior. La lengua no tiene hueso."

"What does that mean, la lengua no tiene hueso," she asked.

"The tongue does not have a bone, so people use it to lie and more. Of course, it's wonderful for kissing." I giggled.

"You're funny, mom. I'm not ready to think beyond tomorrow, mom. This divorce has me on edge. It's one thing or another day after day." She stated as she exhaled smoke.

"Well, I know it has been tough, but you are still so young, and even if you never date again, you still have to start making plans for when you move out of here. Eventually, you will have to start moving out of here, and you will have to begin looking at your future." I said.

"I know, mom, but for the time being, I will bask in today's win!"

"Why don't we get a bottle of champagne as well? We can post that we are celebrating the beginning of a Femi-nazi Club or something." I said.

She laughed so hard for so long tears started rolling down her cheeks. Between the laughter, Maxi would say, "Feminazi power!" and "Proud of it!" Maxi was finally beginning to emerge from the shell this man had stuffed her in. That's the sort of joy I missed seeing in her. Finally, my daughter was coming back to me. Her smile made me laugh too. She was glowing.

Feminazi. This word is used more and more against assertive women. It is the product of one of those television talk shows that pretend to be news in an attempt to subdue strong women. (I suspect it was the fallout of several lawsuits they had to pay out for sexual harassment.) If being assertive is being a Feminazi, then yes, I am a feminazi. If helping your sister, mother, or victim of abuse is being a feminazi, then yes, I am a feminazi. If wanting to have control over my own body means I am a feminazi, then hell yes! I am a feminazi. I want to challenge you and every woman out there to help me hijack this word. Learn to be Feminazi with my Maxi and me. And that's how we take our power back. We emerge stronger.

CHAPTER 8

NON-JUDGMENTAL HEART

I lay in my bed thinking how much Maxi had moved forward in the last couple of months. Still, there were lots of relationships she had to repair. Her sisters needed an explanation for why she was not hanging out with them all these years. They needed to understand what had happened, but it was not the right time. I had to first prepare Maxi for those conversations. She had to apologize for not keeping those lines of communication open. Only, Maxi could sometimes be too proud to do things like that.

Her sisters could be the same. They still had that sibling rivalry, you know, seeking a mother's attention and approval. At times, that can be toxic too. I hoped time had done them good, and they had matured enough to move away from that kind of behavior. It was not going to be easy at all, and it might take quite some time, but first things first. Next, Maxi had to repair the relationship with her aunt and uncle.

I called my brother up and began the healing process for our family. "Hey, manita, how are things going?" He asked on the phone.

"Oh, more of the same. I can't thank you enough for fronting all that money to help Maxi out. As per Maxi, she said Sissy Boy told her you had called him and told him you wanted nothing to do with her. He told her that you two were tired of dealing with her and her issues. I can't imagine anything further from the truth." I said

"Oh! You tell Maxi that that couldn't be further from the truth. I love her and have missed her tons. Let her know that whenever she wants me there, I will be there," he said.

I knew Maxi was listening in from the other room. I had the phone on speaker because I had difficulty hearing the conversations the other way. I wanted her to hear that she was loved, that more people were supporting her than just myself.

"Well, manito, I'm going to see if Maxi is ready to finally see you. It's time we get together again." We said our goodbyes and hung up. Maxi came into the living room and sat down. I could tell she wanted to ask something, but she was likely thinking about how to ask it.

"Hey Mija, I just got off the phone with your tio. He'd really like to see you. You know, he does not hold any grudges."

She looked at me and said, "I know. I'm still just

embarrassed. I just can't believe Sissy Boy was able to push all of you away. He told my family I didn't want to see them and then told me they didn't want to see me because they were tired of putting up with me." She was spiraling through mixed feelings. Feelings I knew all too well.

When abusers isolate a woman, the first thing they do is make her believe no one wants anything to do with them. This is what my first two husbands tried. It is a tactic to remove any power or control we have, so we only look at them. They want to be our only connection to the world, to life itself. If you've ever dealt with an abusive narcissist like Sissy Boy, you know what I mean. You know what it is like to be cut off and feel ashamed to be around people again.

You wonder what they will think of you for being a victim. How could you have let yourself be fooled by a liar? How could you allow them to take so much from you and make you believe anything besides what you already know? So then, when it's time to reconnect, you think that people may truly hold a grudge against you for being gone. I want you to know that you cannot let these thoughts get the better of you. You can always try to reconnect. The people who have always been there for you will welcome you back. If they don't, you don't want them in your new life anyway. They wouldn't be good for you.

That's one more thing you should know about people. Sometimes, people, even friends and family, are fake.

They want you around only when you're useful to them or when they can predict who you'll be. They want you while they can benefit. Once you change—because sometimes life changes you—they leave. It's horrible. But don't think that it is your fault. They left because their love was shallow. They weren't big enough people for you, not because there was something wrong with you.

"Look, Maxi. This is the time when you decide. Will you go back to the family that loves you and cares about you, or you continue being isolated because the emotions of being embarrassed are bigger than you are? Are they? I promise you, Mija, we love you and won't judge you for your ex's behavior? All we want is to continue having you in our lives. This includes your uncle."

Ego. That little voice plants doubt in all we do because it loves to dangle fear in front of us. Letting go of ego is the hardest thing I have ever had to do. Learning to be in silence, without thinking, is a challenge, but I had to learn it to survive. I wonder how many of my readers are being held back by their egos. Breathe in, breathe out, hand-on-heart, and think of nothing. Listen to the beautiful sound of your breath. Don't let your ego in. Keep breathing. This is something I had to do daily as I helped my Maxi out. I took care of myself. But, you see, ego keeps us from taking care of ourselves.

The house was a mess. Maxi had not been feeling well as the stress from the divorce was causing flare-ups. I knew all too well how hard things could be when going through a flare-up. Not to mention that I, too, was beginning to show signs of a flare-up given all the stress. So, I figured it might be time for another story while we waited for my brother to arrive.

As if on cue, Maxi said to me, "Mom, if we are supposed to forgive and try to make things right with our own family, why have you stopped talking to most of your family?"

So here it was, another hard conversation. As I mentioned earlier, I had been gone from the country for well over seven years, and that had caused a rift with my brothers and sisters, or so I thought. Maxi didn't know that her grandmother was very sick and that my brothers, as good old Mexican men do, were pushing for us, the girls in the family, to take care of her. It was the unspoken yet expected thing to do. No regard if we were in a position to do it or not, just do it. They all washed their hands of her except for one brother. He had lived with my mother all his life.

He was only two years younger than me. The best way I could describe their relationship is symbiotic yet toxic. They hated each other, but they put up with each other because no one else could put up with them. For him, it was that he had never truly left the nest. He liked it that way. No rent, no bills, just a free ride. However, he and I did not see eye to eye because I had advised his wife well over twenty years ago to leave him. He was a wife-beater, and she came to me trying to escape from him. The worst part is that they had a daughter, and that beautiful young girl had lived through hell.

The other part of why I didn't care for him was that he took mother's advice to become a wife beater. "Beat her into submission. That's what she needs." Yes, that's the way my mother took care of that. Her boy wasn't getting served like a king, so she gave him the green light to beat her. That's the same thing I saw in Egorr's mother. Hatred for our kind. Women. I never will understand this mentality, and I pray that mothers in all communities change this.

Everyone in town that knew her knew you were not to stand up to my mom because you might just get a slap or a black eye. This five-foot-two stubby woman was a fire-cracker and a possible boxer.

As she lay dying, I tried to visit her. Flew from Korea to be with her, but that was taken away from me. My brother would not "allow" me in mom's house because I would, according to him, bring trouble to mom. Yet, they wanted me to help financially. Can you help with the property taxes, can you send money for the bills, can you, can you... it never stopped. Though I had six brothers and only three sisters, the three sisters and I were burdened with helping. Well, it had been years since I had helped with anything financially. I had put a stop to all that.

As for my mother and I, well, she had wished me dead so many times that I stopped trying to have a relationship with her. According to her, I was why her oldest and most adored son had died. I alone was to be faulted. There was nothing about why he truly died and what had really happened to cause his death. I remember the first time she yelled at me, "I wish you were the one I was burying! You're a witch. The worst thing born to me!"

That first time she spewed those words, I felt like dying. I felt miserable, and it may have been easier if she had just stabbed my heart, but she stabbed me with words. She'd say these things when no one was in the room, and I'm sure my brothers and sisters were beginning to question my sanity as, according to all of them, they had never once heard her say these things. And so, I had to be vulnerable with Maxi so she could see my wounds and hear my story. I was in unchartered water as this was something my culture was against. Secrecy is the preferred methodology in families. I was no longer afraid of speaking my truth. They were.

"Maxi, I have to tell you a little bit more about me. Do you remember when we still lived in Brownsville? There was this huge fight with your grandma and me." I said. She was barely two at the time, and her oldest sister was barely four, so I always wondered if they remembered.

One day in April, my mother came over to my house, where I lived with my second husband, demanding that I give her more money because she was in a bind with some bills. She had three grown men, my brothers, living there with her, and they all worked. Anyway, that's precisely when my husband and I were having marital problems.

On a day he was with his mistress, my mom showed up with my sister-in-law in tow, my brother Lewy's wife. Mom was in one of her moods. The only way I can describe it is that she came into the house nit-picking everything I was doing or had. I knew she was looking for a fight. She had a way of pushing my buttons, and she got what she wanted.

"I had been having nightmares over something that had happened. You see, when I was six years old, my oldest brother began to sexually abuse me. He'd come in drunk at night and come into my room, or I'd be left behind with him alone, and he'd abuse me. This went on for years. I had been struggling with this because we were all girls, and my mother was pissed off at all of us because we would not visit him." I told Maxi.

She and I got into it. She asked for more money, and I was receiving food stamps. I had already given her most of my food stamps. We lived on a third of my income and food stamps just to keep her happy. I decided to say NO to her. I realized that I was not a good mom by limiting our food. So I told her no. This, of course, caused her to have a full-blown meltdown.

"You are a whore. No one will see you for nothing more than a whore! You have kids from two marriages, so you are a whore. You are a disgrace to our family and will never amount to anything!" While she was yelling all these things at me, I began to feel anger toward her for the first time in my life. Before that, I allowed her to do this, and I gave her whatever she wanted to stop all that emotional or physical abuse. It was the year that I turned twenty-five when something clicked in me. I stood up to her like I never thought I would.

I told her, "Yes, mother, I'm a whore because you and your lovely son decided to make me a whore ever since I was six. You think I don't remember what you did?" I was trembling, and she probably thought I was trembling with rage, but I was trembling with fear and a ton of mixed emotions.

Standing up to anyone who abuses you is scary when your heart is kind, or you've learned to be silent and just take the abuse. You hope it will soon stop and go away. These types of human beings feed off of your fear and continue coming at you abusing your kindness. Maxi had to learn to stand up to her abuser as I had to learn to stand up to mine. There's nothing wrong with saying no to your abusers. My long journey in life has taught me as much. Now I had to tell the one truth that hurt the most. I had to once again be vulnerable and teach my Maxi there's nothing wrong with standing up for yourself or being vulnerable.

Because my sister-in-law was there, mom had to play innocent to prevent our family secret from getting out. She began to get up and yell more hurtful things, "You are a crazy bitch! Do you hear the crazy shit this bitch is saying! You are no daughter of mine! How dare you say things about your brother! Let's go!" As she was yelling all this, she gathered her things and walked out the door. Finally, I had the guts to tell her, "If I'm no longer your daughter, then I don't want to see you here ever again! Don't come begging for money or anything else. Oh, and you know that what I'm saying is the truth! You know all too well, and one day you and your son will have to answer to God!" I don't know how I got all the strength and courage to tell her off like that, but deep down inside, something told me I had to do this. That day and night, I cried for myself as I had never cried before. I sat inside the closet, holding my knees and rocking myself. What I had done had rocked my very core. I prayed and prayed for God to heal me. I guess he heard my prayer because the very next day, all hell broke loose.

I never once said which brother had sexually been abusing me for years. Apparently, after this, my sister-in-law went to her husband and demanded to know who had done this to me. So, of course, he had to come out and say who had done this and the fact that he had also been abused because my mom was playing this game of "forgetting" how she allowed our brother to abuse us. Forgetting how she initiated it all. I was the youngest female, and she would fondle me in front of Will, laughing at my vagina. I remember waking up when I was three because I was listening to her and him as she pulled on my panties and fondled me. He would laugh. He was nineteen at the time, and I was three...three.

He had also tried to abuse my oldest sisters, and that's the reason they left as soon as they could. I think my oldest sister was eighteen, and my other sister was sixteen at the time. I was four when they left. They ended up joining the Job Corps just to get out of the house. Never returned but to visit maybe five times, if that during the time I still lived with mom. But, the important piece of all this is that both of my oldest sisters knew he was dangerous. They did nothing about it. I get that at the time, they were young and did not know what to do, and that's why I have forgiven them in my heart, but there was no way I could have a meaningful relationship with them, especially after I found out as an adult that one of my sisters had worked in Texas with Child Protective Services. That moment tore into me like a knife. To this day, that part of my story hurts so much.

Unfortunately, that sister ended up re-victimizing me by trying to shift the blame on me. I voiced my need to go to counseling with her, but she declined, and that was the end of that. I can't imagine that she feels guilt at all as she said as much. I call her 'Mrs. Perfect' because she constantly speaks about how she had the sense to get out and create her own perfect life. Now, I need you to keep in mind that they were adults in their twenties and thirties, and I was still a child. Even after all that, I was willing to work on our relationship, but she wasn't. That's when I realized that I had never truly had that sisterly love. She threw me out and was not willing to work on our relationship. It took me many months to accept my reality.

Not long after that big altercation with my mother at my house, according to my younger brother, Roland, she called the eldest and began to have "the conversation" that evening. As I'm told, it went something like this.

"Well, your sister is saying you sexually abused her." She said while she was sucking on a cigarette as if it would give her what she wanted. He, of course, negated everything and even said to her, "If I did anything that they are accusing me of, may God take my life." I'm told my mom responded with, "Well, if it's true, I curse you, and may God take your life dragging you to hell like the dog you are!"

All I can say is that it's very clear in the good book that we cannot take God's name in vain. The very next day, around three or four in the afternoon, my brother Lewy came to the house and told me Will had died, and mom wanted to see me. When he told me this, he was standing outside of the screen door of my house, and I just stood there in shock. Thinking that maybe he was pulling my leg and that this was all a sick joke, so I would take everything back, but it was not. In my eyes, God had had enough of those two and gave them exactly what they had asked for.

After all that had happened and to that funeral, going to my mother's house was the hardest day of my life. To that point, my older sisters had never had a reason to have any form of relationship with me. They'd call home regularly and send stuff by mail, but they never really talked to me. So, when this happened, they somehow got my number because they wanted to know all the details of what had happened. I now realize that all they wanted was to circulate my life story amongst them and how I had been brave enough to finally speak up. They also wanted to feed their anger against my mother, which I understood to some degree. For years I allowed them to keep it up because I wanted them in my life so badly that I never saw that they were just basking in the past. Constantly picking at their wounds and at mine.

My other brothers, though, were just confused about everything. Remember, they still lived with my mom, and she had their ear. She began claiming that I was working the "streets" as a prostitute and things like that. She'd make claims about me being seen in Mexican bars and such. Just awful things. So then she'd say that all of what I was saying was not true because what was really going on was that I was trying to cover up my evil ways as a prostitute.

After the shock wore off, I went to mom's house, and there she was, crying. I'm very sure her pain for Will was real. That, I will never question. But once I arrived, she saw me and did something I never expected. She hugged me and began crying that she was so sorry for everything that had happened. Then your aunts and uncles walked out of the room to give us a moment to ourselves, and... that's the very first time she told me she wanted me dead and decided I had been the one that killed her beloved son.

From what I've pieced together. The day after the big fight, my brother, who was in Tennessee, had been working in the fields. He began to complain about a stomach ache to his wife. Then during lunchtime, they all sat up against the big tractors, and he began to grab his chest and yell weird things like, "No, don't take me! I'm sorry! I don't want to go with you!" He had begun rolling around on the dirt and somehow ended up under one of the trucks. When they finally were able to pull him from under the truck, he was dead. Heart attack at forty. Only God knows what he was seeing. I've prayed for his soul because I can't bring myself to judge him harshly as he was yet another victim of abuse.

————

Maxi and I sat in silence for what felt a long time. We both were lost in our own thoughts. I thought about how people tend to walk away from families like ours. They know ugly stuff is happening. The saddest part about it all is that, to this day, people believe that children that are abused end up abusing others. That is not at all accurate. As new studies come out, they are finding that fewer adults of sexual abuse actually end up abusing. It's basic common sense. Those that are hurt know how it feels so they typically don't hurt others the same way they were hurt. I'm not saying that abused children never abuse. However, we need to be clear as to the true numbers here. Did you know that only 35% of males that are sexually abused end up abusing? And less than 1% of females end up sexually abusing others. I remember hearing and learning that all abusers were likely abused. We need to stop saying that because it's not helpful, and it's actually one of the reasons victims don't speak up. I know that's one of the reasons it took me so long to speak up.

I have forgiven my brother, and I have peace about all this because I know my brother was also a victim. Except his abuse was from a mother who likely didn't know doing those things to me was hyper-sexualizing him. I honestly believe that the internet is having the same effect on young minds. Porn. The hyper-sexualization of future pedophiles. That, it is my belief, is the other 65% of men who are out there raping children. That's my belief because of the many porn magazines my brother had in his room for years.

I think humanity is still very young in the psychology department when it comes to dealing with family dynamics and the complications abuse brings. Don't get me wrong; we are getting better at understanding the effects as we continue to beat the drum asking those that are dealing with mental anguish to seek help. Judging others when they are in crisis is despicable. The worst part is that many families have similar devastating abuse that they deal with by trying to hide it. They will call the victim a liar. They will push the victim away. I guess it's easier to pretend that victim is crazy than to deal with the family skeletons.

This type of behavior only pushes victims deeper into their little hole of despair. It isolates them and keeps them from getting the proper help they need. Then there's the shaming that happens if a victim seeks help.

Many families still believe that seeking proper psychological help means that you must be crazy and would disgrace the family. I believe that's what happened to Egorr, and that's what happens to many of you. Stop allowing those that surround you or your ego to stop you from seeking proper mental help.

I've learned to be proud of the fact that I'm a survivor and not a victim. I wanted Maxi to be proud of what she was accomplishing by getting back her self-worth. It's a hard lesson to learn for a person that survives abuse. Learning to not allow others to abuse you can be challenging once you go through any kind of abuse. You fear judgment by others because your abuser has judged you all along. Belittled you. Slowly chipping away at your self-worth. Keeping you from becoming a better form of yourself. They make you believe you are nothing without them, and you begin to believe that. Just like my Maxi had been made to believe this, I, too, believed this for most of my life.

Maybe other people cover their pain well, but I don't. I am who I am because of everything I've lived through. I would not change anything about myself because I love myself just as God created me. If a person wants to judge me for my past, good riddance! Adios!

Getting out of a dysfunctional marriage should be celebrated. The amount of women that still buy into old ideas of staying in dysfunctional marriages amazes and pains me. I know there are men out there that are good men. They truly take care of their daughters and wives. I celebrate those men and the women that raised them.

I was still stuck in my thoughts when I realized my shirt was wet because Maxi was quietly crying. I don't know how long I had been caught in my own thoughts after telling my truth. I looked down at her and saw her wiping the tears off her face. She cleared her throat and said, "Mom, I don't think I could ever be as strong as you've had to be in life."

I pushed her away and grabbed her by her shoulders gently, and said, "Mija, life has a way of teaching us whatever we need out of it. It's a journey we all go through. Life lessons are handed out in-discriminatorily. No one chooses to have these hard moments in life. Remember, by the time I was being sexually abused, I had found my life vest in that tent church. God knew I would need him."

The doorbell rang, and I quickly got up to answer it. It was Roland. He was so eager to see Maxi that he quickly hugged me and, in a couple of strides, made it to Maxi. He made her stand up from the couch and hugged her with so much love that I could not help but tear up. He was not judging her, just holding her with all the love and care she deserved. Maxi was full-blown crying by then. It was the most beautiful time we had together. I knew things were only going to get better from this point forward. Maxi was getting back into our small family, and she'd only grow and learn from all that had happened to her. Just like I had. Just like you will.

CHAPTER 9

CHAIN LINK

The weeks passed by slowly. It was already February, and Texas was in its second week under a snowstorm. My emotional self was feeling great because I knew that as long as this snowstorm persisted, the likelihood of Sissy Boy showing up at Maxi's house was almost incredibly low. The streets were frozen, and it kept snowing. Austin was not prepared for weather like this, but for Maxi and me, it was a Godsend.

We called each other twice, sometimes three times a day. She was beginning to box her clothing and shoes. We sang songs about hope and the future. About being strong and not giving up. My girl had weathered the worst part of the separation. Still, I felt uneasy because a date had been set for mediation. Hopefully, everything could be agreed on. After that, the divorce would be a matter of simply separating the assets and each party going their separate way. Sissy Boy was so stuck trying to screw Maxi over and leave her destitute that his rage blinded him.

On the other hand, Maxi had the upper hand, given the abuse she had endured. My heart ached when she told me the full story about how he raped her. To think that there are men out there who still believe they can force their wives into any kind of sexual activity, even if she says "No." These men make it hard for women to progress and trust. They are the ones who create conflict between men and women when there should be a union.

I sat next to my living room window, wondering the type of upbringing Sissy Boy would have had to imagine he could just force himself on my girl. Apparently, on the day this happened, some of Maxi's life-long friends had been downstairs while he "had" her upstairs. Her friends knew when Maxi and Sissy Boy came downstairs that something was wrong with Maxi.

I can only report on what Maxi told me said because I wasn't there—and they're all lucky I wasn't. The things she told me made my blood boil. How could any person be so disgusting and evil? To take another person's body and violate their consent. Married or not, this is never tolerable. This alone makes him unforgivable, and it hurts me more knowing that the relationship did not end there. What did he have on her to make her stay after this? My daughter...

Her friends took her to a doctor, and she had to be sewn. Unfortunately, she did not make a proper police report. Our attorney did take depositions of her friends.

Her friends had not returned to her house since that incident. They told her they feared for her safety and that she had a place to stay if she ever needed to run from him. Sissy Boy stood firm in claiming they were just experimenting, and she was exaggerating.

All I could do as a mother was a hug and hold my child as close to me as I could. The tears rolled from both of us many times as she expressed herself. My heart would ache with unbearable pain, yet hate for that monster made me commit to ensuring my girl was cared for!

It was then that I knew I had to push her hard to continue going to counseling. She had been, and it showed as she slowly revealed the nightmare she had endured. Why do women do this? Women give men too many chances, and it is time for a change. Shame on mothers and fathers who don't teach their sons limitations. Take, take, take. That's what they teach their sons. Disgusting.

Once Sissy Boy's parents had gotten wind about this, they were determined to get involved in the divorce. No surprise there. They showed up with their son to meetings. They decided to start saying that the house was not sold to their son, but rather he was leasing from them, and as such, they wanted Maxi out of the house. Once that February freeze was over, they served Maxi with an eviction letter.

The phone rang, and there she was again. Crying yet furious about the ability of these evil people to do such a thing. As a mother, I understood why they were doing all this, but I would make sure my daughter would come out of this with as many assets as possible. So, we began to fight back even harder.

Her attorney had made it clear that she had no recourse because there was no physical evidence of an agreement, and the house was under his parents' name. So we got to work. We found as much information on evictions as possible. Apparently, because of COVID, there was a moratorium on evictions. We printed the response to the eviction, pointed out that there was a moratorium, and sent it to their mansion. Almost immediately, he began calling her and threatening that she'd end up with absolutely nothing if she kept it up. The judge had made it clear that he could NOT limit her access to the bank accounts. They had settled on a set amount of monthly money to be given to my daughter. He made about five figures a month but wanted to give her something like $1000 a month. Her medication alone costs well over $1000. So, he would say, "She is not disabled. She's just lazy and wants to live like a queen." But, of course, her attorney had gotten the medical records and testimony from her doctors that proved otherwise. This, by the end, would end up being a huge hammer that her attorney would use in combination with the laws that exist about abuse against disabled individuals.

My daughter received illegal eviction notices with threats of locking her out, and month by month, we'd respond. Given that the monthly amount had been settled, my daughter was able to begin to get things ready for the inevitable move. The entire process began to reveal how narcissistic and abusive Egorr really was. Then his parents began coming into the house unannounced. Since they claimed to be landlords, they thought they could enter the house unannounced to take pictures. They were trying to use the "mess" that my girl had in the house as evidence that they needed to have her removed. They failed, though. The "mess," as they called it, were the many boxes Maxi was already using to pack her things.

The parents went as far as to make it seem that they had hired an attorney. I took one look at the "legal" looking letter and was quickly able to find that it was actually from a kit that could be purchased from a law firm in Houston. We had filed against them for coming into the house without proper notification by that point. They were sent a cease-and-desist letter from the proper authorities, and sure enough, it all stopped. However, the phone calls and the stupidity of what Sissy Boy would say were beyond skeptical. By that time, it was May. Finally, they did do things right. They set up an eviction notice with the proper authorities and gave Maxi a month to move out.

However, we responded by letting them know we would go ahead and show up in court to discuss the housing issue. Maxi had gotten Sissy Boy to admit that the house was supposed to be their house and not a lease. She had learned to record him every single time he called. We pointed that out in the letter and sent

them the legal information from Texas about commit-
ting this kind of fraudulent act. We further stated that
Maxi would request that she needed to stay in the house
until there was a split of assets so she could use the
money to move and find housing for herself. They realized they had been stupid because Google is not a law
firm. By that time, I had been living with her. I'd run to
my house and stay one night to ensure things were
alright and then take off the next morning as early as
possible.

I was anxious as I was about to start a job in late July,
and if they could not agree, I'd likely have to give up my
job to be here with my girl. Finally, a date was set for the
first week of June. I was hopeful things would be worked
out, and Maxi would get more than half of the assets.
That day, I was next to the phone. Praying.

"Lord, I'm not asking for my girl to leave that man
with nothing. I'm just asking that she be taken care of to
move on. Be just with her, please." The calls would come
in whenever they were on a break, and she'd tell me what
was going on. His parents were there with him but had
been banned from going into the room where the medi-
ator and the attorneys were working on an agreement if at
all possible. From what Maxi told me, they could not
believe he brought his parents to the meeting.

"Mom, you won't believe what he's fighting about. He
wants to keep all my pets. Can you believe it! He wants us
to split them. He keeps Sissy, her dog, and a cat, and I get
one of the cats. Can you believe that? The attorney is

asking if I have any evidence these pets were mine before the marriage. Do I, mom?" she asked nervously.

I looked for anything in my emails, and her sisters did the same. One of her sisters sent an affidavit for the kitten. She had given it to her several months prior and had documented this in texts. So the kitten was Maxi's. Then her older cat. I found the adoption papers and took a picture of them. She was Maxi's as well. Then it was Sissy. Sissy was a gift from Sissy Boy to her when they were dating. Maxi found the text messages and gave them to her attorney. Sissy was safe with Maxi as well. The day continued with this and that. They tried to lowball Maxi with the amount, and finally, her attorney took the big hammer out. She gave Maxi permission to tell her stories of the abuse. Then her attorney presented the medical information and the affidavits from several doctors and Maxi's friends. SLAM DUNK!

Ultimately, through mediation, they were able to agree. Maxi received her fair share of assets and got to keep her pets. She had two weeks to finish packing and get out of the house. I had already prepared my house to receive her. I was not prepared, however, with the number of boxes and things she had. She was finally free of Sissy Boy.

We packed away through the next two weeks and prepared for the move. I was already working by the time she moved into my house. Everyone in my family came together to help her move. It was good to have her safe and sound in my house.

I'm stopping here to say that what my girl endured may likely be something you can relate to. Divorce is hard enough without people fighting over things simply to hurt one another. Divorcing a narcissist is hard because they want to hurt you, and they keep at it by trying to throw you off balance. Egorr tried by demanding to keep the pets away from my Maxi. He knew they helped her, given her disability. He never cared for the pets; he just wanted to hurt her. When something like this happens, you have to stop and use your breathing techniques. Don't give way to anxiety. Stay calm. This is when you must keep going and focus on what IS important to you. Don't allow the feelings of betrayal to get the best of you. I know those feelings all too well, and now, so does my girl. You have to remind yourself that you are almost at the end and will get through it.

How do I know this? The loneliness I felt having to go through my divorces on my own at such a young age was isolating. Not to mention societies and my own families backlash for not conforming to what was expected of me. So, I got angry with everyone. Maybe you, too, are angry, and you want to isolate yourself even further. I didn't isolate myself after my second divorce. With the help of a psychologist, I finally learned it was healthy to date. Talk about breaking the norms of my culture! My point is that though it may not feel like it, you are at that moment when you break free. Don't be scared. There will be a better tomorrow. Soon enough.

The weeks went by, and I noticed Maxi would sleep a

lot. Just like I did when Lupus had been at its worst. I was
so worried for her. I had installed cameras around my
house and would monitor the house to make sure Sissy
Boy would not show up with that gun. Though her
divorce agreement ensured her location was hidden, I still
worried. Why? All studies show that abused women run
the highest risk of being murdered when they leave their
abuser. So I was not taking any chances.

I had a friend, Mike, who would drive by and make
sure all was fine in the house daily while I was at work.
Mike quickly became Maxi's friend as well. He was this
rough older man who lacked all his teeth, but somehow, it
fit him. He was tough and would say what was on his
mind without thinking twice. Maxi needed so much affir-
mation, especially from men, and he gave her that. I knew
as much because I hadn't had that since my dad passed
away when I was fourteen.

When I would get home, I would find her in the backyard sitting with a cigarette in hand. She was smoking
less, but at times she still smoked four or five cigarettes in
one sitting. I knew she was feeling uneasy about her
future.

"Mom, what's going to happen to me? I don't want to
live here all my life and depend on you. I don't want to be
like that brother of yours that lived all his life with
grandma."

Slowly, I guided Maxi to take care of all her medical
needs before her insurance ran out. COVID was
becoming a blessing in disguise. Egorr, it was agreed upon,

would have to continue including her on his insurance until the final divorce decree. Because of COVID, there was a good possibility her decree wouldn't be finalized until at least two, maybe three months after mediation. As any mother would, I urged Maxi to continue forward with two minor operations she had to have. Time was running out, but she was able to get both operations before her insurance ran out. She was even able to get a much-needed dentist visit in.

Despite all of this progress, this was still a difficult period in Maxi's life. Things were happening so fast; I believe her emotional self didn't have time to keep up with it all because she began doubting her future even more. She became irritable, and she started sleeping for most of the day. I watched as she slowly fell into depression. Admittedly, this was something I wasn't well prepared to deal with. I don't think anyone is until they've been through it at least once. Still, I could relate to it, somewhat, because given the years I spent in bed sick and depending on others for many things, I, too, had been depressed. I knew that the one thing that helped me the most was to begin setting goals. So, I pushed Maxi to do as much.

First, I strategized how I would approach her. I knew that people suffering from depression aren't in their regular minds and don't process input the same. I wanted to be motherly and supportive and still encourage her to take action and get out of it. The strong woman in me wanted to see her rise. The first thing I figured she would need is to feel like she has a place to belong and a reason to get up. She needed community. I began by ensuring she would have people she could talk to during the day and rely on. Mike and his wife were just the people Maxi needed to be around.

I loved seeing Mike at times. He was such a character. Tall, skinny, sickly, just like us. We related to each other so well. His wife, who normally hung in the truck, was the quiet type. I introduced Maxi to this odd couple, and they hit it off. Mike would come around and start some of his crazy stories. Sometimes I wondered if they were real or if he was just trying to get us to laugh, but it was working. Maxi was slowly getting out of her depressive mood.

"So, how are you liking our town, Maxi? Quite the place, ain't it? Crooked cops, shifty neighbors, and the three restaurants in town are to die for. No, literally if you eat there, you might die." He laughed, and his wife said, "Yup!"

Not only did Mike, his wife, and Maxi hit it off, but they helped us out in times of need. Since I was already working, Maxi didn't want to compromise my job when she needed to go to Austin for her surgeries. So, the odd couple would step in and help us out. I could hear Maxi's voice getting stronger. I could feel Maxi's spirit lifting every time someone stepped in to help her. Slowly but surely, she began to get out of her funk. Eventually, more hard questions came for me.

"So mom, I see why you had to cut ties with your family, but I still feel that maybe there's more there.

What else happened? How could you continue feeling bad for them after all that has happened to your mom?"

"Well, I can't say it's easy, and we all need some form of family around us."

Like I had told Maxi before, if we don't have some form of family, we have to create our own. I feel that my mom lacked so many tools in her life because she did not have her mother to teach her love and empathy. Empathy is what we lack in the world more than ever before. I honestly believe that if you behave badly, guilt will get you. I've seen it one too many times. Guilt has a way of eating away at a person's soul. No matter how much a person may try to be non-caring, not including narcissistic folks here, they know when they've wronged someone, and it will eat at them. Just take Will, my brother: his heart gave up when confronted with his truth. The same with my mother. Her little secret of possibly poking that horse's ass ate at her. Back in her time, children were not given counseling. It wasn't even a thing. So they had to be tough in the face of life's many challenges.

I always imagine a little girl confused and wondering if her mother had died of the "fake" disease or if maybe the horse falling on her stomach caused her death. That consumed her, but she was unwilling to talk about it. Instead, she stuffed it in her TNT box, and it kept going off. Explosions of anger daily and, at times, several times a day. Then there were the obsessions we endured. Every day my mother would get up and work cleaning the house. The things she did to clean that house were, now I know, out of the ordinary. I now laugh at many of the things she had us do but living through them was awful.

We had to "Spring clean" the house at least three times per year, sometimes four times. We all hated the cleaning. I've said many times that she could have run the Army better than any man there. Cleaning day usually started at around five in the morning or six if we were lucky. The first task was to take all the bedsheets, curtains, and tablecloths and wash everything. While the beds were undone, we had to clean every little part of them. The screws, the railings, the headboard, and the footboards. We'd take the bed mattresses out into the hallway and ensure they had no stains. If they did, she'd put together some cleaning concoction. Unfortunately, she often put together chemicals that don't belong together—like ammonia and Clorox (do NOT mix!)—forcing us to run out of the house coughing. Occasionally, I was grateful for those mishaps because they provided much-needed breaks. Still, sometimes we were forced to put on a handkerchief over our mouth and nose to continue working.

Once the buckets of her cleaning concoction were in each room, we'd begin tackling every little thing in the room. The figurines were the one thing I hated. She'd go room to room checking on our work. Inspecting the figurines making sure they were glistening, she'd look in the tiny little holes to ensure they had been cleaned. Of course, you did not want to get anything wrong, or the broomstick would come down on your head. Those little holes in the bottom of the fucking figurines earned me several bruises. I can relate to those cartoons where the characters see stars or little birds after getting hit.

You also have to remember that we were not rich by any means. My dad would work from before the sun came up until sundown to try and feed and dress all the kids my mom kept popping out. So before you ask me where he was, that's where he was most of the days except on weekends. Weekends were my favorite time because mom would try to keep her cool as long as he was there.

Then came the floor. We cleaned the floor the Cinderella way, with a bucket next to each of us and some scrubbing tools. She'd stand over us and would point out every scuff mark. They had to be gone before we'd create more. Once we moved the bed and the furniture back into each room, I always thought we would create more and we'dbe back on our knees. Once the floor was done, we'd move the furniture back in and scrub those scuff marks. She would make sure the set-up of the bedrooms always changed. We could not set up the bed in the same place it used to be. After everything was put back together and the ceiling, light bulbs, windows, and walls were freed of any dust or cobwebs, it was time to get the drawers fixed. Mom was so particular about how things looked in each drawer. The underwear had to be folded in neat little squares, and the socks had to be tied together. She had stopped tucking them into each other because they would become too loose, and my brothers would complain. Of course, my brothers were not helping inside.

They had the whole yard and the storage rooms to clean up. So, my mom had an army of kids just cleaning everything in that awful house.

One year, sometime after Dad passed away, she had another idea. She had ordered my brothers NOT to throw out the oil from when they did the oil changes from her truck, so we had all of this oil in storage. So that summer, she decided that instead of buying the Old English furniture oil, she'd just use the car oil to save money. Yes, I know...

Sometimes people do things that we might not find very bright, but it turned out to be the brightest idea yet. That year we polished the walls, the floor, and the furniture with gobs and gobs of motor oil. The smell was horrible for days. I kept thinking that if she dropped any of her cigarettes, we would likely go up in flames, but we did not, thank God! It actually helped when our home was flooded happened later that year.

It was 1982, and I was still in high school when the flood happened. It rained for days without stopping, and our neighborhood was the most vulnerable and damaged because of the location. Our community and many others, mostly the poor and disenfranchised, had been built on land that used to be old lakes that cities in south Texas had decided to fill with dirt and sell as "cheap land." So when it rained, the water gathered and pooled at our doorsteps. In desperation, and mostly because I feared going back home because I knew my mother would be enraged as never before, I volunteered for the Red Cross as an interpreter and later with FEMA. I helped all our people navigate the applications they had to fill out once FEMA designated the event as a federal disaster.

Fear of additional abuse by my mother propelled me to learn something about myself. I could effectively affect outcomes if I set my mind to it. I learned about the power of media as I would invite the media over to see the devastation. This helped me become an activist of sorts. The city manager and all the city council had failed us. We were the forgotten ones. They had decided to cut expenditure on something vital to our community. Pumps. Pumps that used to keep those neighborhoods from flooding had been cut off the budget. Canal systems had been ignored and not cleaned out.

During a meeting with the mayor and the council in city hall, with hundreds of people inside and outside and cameras rolling from major news sources, I spoke up and began to assert myself. At this moment, life and fear showed me the power of speaking up. The power of standing up for those in need. The power of standing up to those that abuse us. I was learning to take my power back in one small way, and it felt so good!

The mayor tried to gaslight us by saying, "Your people throw trash in the canals, and that's why this happened."

With a loud and proud voice, I said, "And my people pay taxes too."

Then he had the gall to say, "Most of your people can't vote because they aren't citizens."

This lit a fire of indignation in me that I had never felt

before. How dare this power-hungry fat HISPANIC man who had been mayor for close to twenty years talk to me this way? How could he talk about us this way? How could he be so indignant?

"Yes, you are absolutely right," I said. "Many of my people aren't citizens of this country, but I am, and so are most of the children they have here. So are most of the seniors about to be eighteen, and mark my word, as God is my witness, I will make sure you are voted out in the next election."

This is how I learned to stand up for myself. To fight for what's right. I was barely sixteen years old. The following year, when he was up for re-election, I rallied the community against him, and he was voted out of office. I kept my promise. Change doesn't happen unless we stand up tall and speak up loudly. I loved helping other people from our neighborhood, and it earned me one of those medals from Washington.

Once the flooding and some of the excitement had subsided, it was time to fix up our home. Our house was in the lowest part of the neighborhood, and water had been standing in our house for all that time well. The muck that was left once the water subsided was unimaginable. The streets were littered with dead fish, feces, and who knows what else, and it wasn't much different inside. Luckily, the flood did not hurt the walls or the floor because everything was polished with the motor oil. So, mom brought in the bright green lawn hose and began hosing down the walls and floor, every room, every crevice, until the house was "clean." That was the first time she had ever done it, but it became a regular ritual on the cleaning days. Now I realize this was a form of PTSD. There was no mental help at the time. All we could do was cope with her behavior and try not to get her mad.

When we got to that bathroom, she'd grab that hose as if her life depended on it. She'd have the youngest brother outside the window, put the hose in through the tiny bathroom window, and yell, "Turn it on!" She'd kink the hose and have one of us scrub down the toilet. The outside of the toilet would always look like it was brand new, but then she'd stick the hose into the toilet. She'd shove that hose as far as she could and say, "Those pipes need to be cleaned out because otherwise, we might end up with a backed-up toilet." I honestly think our house likely had the cleanest sewer pipes in the world.

The year that the toilet was finally replaced, we all stood and looked into the hole where the pipe came up, and you won't believe that the pipes looked brand new! Then, my brother-in-law, the one who changed the toilet, asked if we had replaced all the pipes. We giggled, of course, and said, "No, we just clean them."

I know it's not funny to say that our mother had all those mental problems, but you know, many folks in our community and in the world do odd things like my mom. They are likely lost in their past or victims of trauma that's never properly been dealt with. They never got a chance to work on themselves to come to some form of self-forgiveness or understanding. So they end up doing things like this.

Hosing the house down was a traumatic memory for me for a long time, but it has become a symbol of resilience. The essential parts of our home weren't destroyed, so we were able to wash the muck away. It can be this way in life, too. As long as the essential parts of you are not destroyed, you can wash the crap that builds up. You can pick yourself up and create a fresh start, even deep in the midst of a crisis.

Now that you are about to move to a different chapter in your life. You have to make sure you resolve your past. Truly resolve it. Do the hard work. Move forward and think about the good things that marriage brought you. It was, at first, a good marriage. You two had wonderful times. Forgive your partner for the hurt he or she caused you, but don't forget it, as it's one of those life lessons you might not want to repeat as I did. Learn from those lessons. Move forward and do it with gusto. You have so much to look forward to. So many possibilities. This is an exciting time in your life, just like it was about to be for my Maxi.

Maxi and I thought we were at a safe place by this point in our journey. We were working on strengthening our bond. By telling her about my mother's past, her many faults, my faults, and my divorces, I was helping her to accept that some things in life are complicated. Sometimes, there is no ONE person to blame for a situation. Things just go wrong. This is a stark turn from blaming herself and then from blaming Egorr. Yes, he was to blame for his actions as an adult. But when you pull back and look at the big picture, his problems didn't start with him. Nor did mine or my mothers. When we can accept this, chains are broken, and we can choose the ones we want to repair and keep close to us.

CHAPTER 10

BREAKING OFF OR TIGHTENING THE LINK

Weeks went by, and I was feeling stressed by all the boxes all over the house. Maxi had barely done anything to try and make our house comfortable. She was still spending way too much time in bed. However, her operation was healing nicely, and that's all that mattered.

"Mija, do you think you could maybe try and condense some of these boxes? Maybe we can call your cousin to come out here and help us." I was beginning to sound a little more snappy because work had become chaotic, to say the least.

Coming back to Texas to teach had been the worst idea in my career. I should have known that teaching in the states in a public school would not be like in Korea. The lack of actual books in the classrooms and the amount of documentation that had to be kept up for each student was totally foolish. I had to put the same information in three different spreadsheets or programs. I did not understand the repetition of the information. I was stressed out because I had forty-one students divided into two blocks, but I loved my third-grade students. They were low due to the amount of time they had spent away from school due to COVID. So, my stress levels were going up, and I was not as understanding with my daughter. I began to resent that she would sleep all day and be awake most of the night. Finally, I had to say something to her.

"Mija, I need to have a serious conversation with you. I need to get to my boxes. I need some of my teaching tools. Do you think you could begin working on those boxes? I come home, and you are asleep. I worry that you are depressed."

"Mom, give me a break! I've been here what, two months! I need to sort things out slowly!" She responded.

"OK, Mija. It's just that I'm having a hard time at work, and I really need to get to my things. I'm not trying to start anything with you."

"I know, I know. You probably want me gone already!"

Where was all this coming from? I had had a really bad day, and there she was, behaving like a teen again. So, I told her, "Well, if you are thinking of moving out already, please let me know when so I can make plans around all that." I did not understand why she was in such a bad mood, or maybe it was me. "I knew you were going to pull this shit on me! My sisters have been warning me that you would ask me to leave soon enough!" and there it was. The rumor mill. Always at the root of these problems.

"I'm sure you want to have your own place and would also want to begin your life. Do what you have to do. All I'm asking is for you to be understanding with me. I can't cook, I can't sit at my desk, there are boxes everywhere!" I was beginning to lose my patience. "Mija, I want to help you, and you do not understand me.

"Whatever, mom! It's always the same thing with you!"

"You know what, Maxi, start looking for a place. I've been nothing but nice to you, and I don't understand why you're not even trying to see my point of view! You have to move out eventually and begin your life. Start looking for work or apply for disability. I've told you I'd help you, but you refuse. I can't do it all and then be kicked for helping! So you know what, start looking for a place!"

She walked outside to smoke. I had lost my temper. Here she was in her thirties, and she did not have the sense to understand how hard things were for me as well. I did not like it when I'd lose control like that, and it was as if my mom would take over. I bitched about everything and allowed my stress to go out the door. "I come home, and I have to clean after you. You don't even rinse the cups. I wash your clothes, I feed you, and you disrespect me like this. No, Mija, that's not right for you to do! If you want to go, then go. I'm not stopping you. Just remember, now you have all that money in the bank, and suddenly you've decided to treat me like shit! Nope, I'm not about to put up with that, so start looking!"

I went into my room, grabbed Opal, and started getting ready for bed. I was exhausted from work. I lay there thinking that I had gone over the top, but I knew her well enough to know that she needed to hear tough truths once in a while. I wondered if she was going to finally start her life. I prayed that she would get out of that funk she was under and begin moving forward. Another month of her smoking and lying in bed, wearing the same clothes day in and day out was not going to happen. I also knew that the hospital had prescribed her those awful pain medications. They usually cause a person to be mean and shit. That night, I did not sleep much, and by six in the morning, I was already in my car heading to work.

That evening I came home to find Maxi had cleaned up some. She had moved some boxes from the couch, and I could finally sit and do some of my work there. She came up to me and apologized. I apologized to her too and told her that though I had yelled at her, I still loved her and wanted her to begin looking to the future.

"Yes, Mija, you can begin taking more pills for depression, but you first have to put some effort into life. If you need to take medication to get out from under that depressive mood you've been under, then so be it, but you have to move out of that bed. I know it's tough, but if you don't begin moving, I'm coming home to find you stuck to those bedsheets one day. I'll have to use the pancake flipper to flip you over." She giggled. "I'm being serious, Maxi. You have to begin sorting your life. Mija, to me, you don't want to move forward. You want to stay in the nest. I wish I could keep you in this nest, but I'm your mom, and I have to make sure the day I'm gone from this earth, you will be able to take care of yourself. Plus, the toughest part is over. The next part is the fun part. Reinvent yourself."

"But mom, who's going to want to hire me? I'm constantly sick and having to go to the doctors and all that!" She said with tears in her eyes. The pain she felt was marked in her trembling voice. Uncertain of that future. I knew the feeling so well. Every time I had to make major changes in my life, I had the same fears, but I had not allowed them to linger in me for too long. At a very young age, I learned that the faster you begin moving forward toward a goal, the faster you'd resolve whatever issue. How would I help her move forward? Make her see that she could begin that process? How could I make her see that once she moved forward, she'd become stronger? As a mom, I knew that I would have to kick her out if she did not begin her life. Like birds in a nest, there's always that one little bird who fears the world. It was time to push my girl a little bit further toward the edge of the nest.

"Well, Mija, are you ready to move forward? I mean, I know it's a scary thought, but unless you begin applying for jobs or deciding what you want for your future, nothing will happen. I can't have you just sitting around wasting away your most valuable years. Who knows, maybe you'll find love again?"

"I will never date again, mom!"

"Ay, Mija, I know you are still hurting from this divorce. However, look at what you've accomplished. You kicked his ass to the curb! You stood up to his family! You fought for what was rightfully yours, and you ended up winning! Do you realize how much you have already accomplished? Now you are here, resting from it all. I get it. I wish I would have been able to stop and rest too, but I've learned that the faster you begin working toward a goal, the faster you will heal. I promise you, Mija, someone out there will give you a job and treat you right. You are so smart and capable. I know because I've seen you at your best and your worst. When you are on, you are amazing. We need to turn you back on! How about we go out shopping? I know shopping always makes me feel better. I need some pants and shirts for work because what I have is quite old now. What do you say? Let's plan a day out there in Austin for shopping, maybe this Saturday?

I saw her thinking about it. She usually frowned and perked up her lips to one side when deep in thought. "OK, mom, but please don't get up super early. How about at twelve or one?" she asked as she scratched her head. "Sure, but I'm coming into your room to wake you up and get you going if you're not up by around eleven in the morning."

That Saturday, I was up by nine in the morning. Cleaning up and getting myself ready. Making as much noise as I could so that Maxi could start waking up. I started the coffee maker and made breakfast. By then, I had done the dishes and had served myself breakfast. I figured at around ten-thirty, I would open her door to let her pets out. Sissy would need to go out, and the cats likely needed to use the cat litter. I also knew that Opal would begin chasing the cats around. All that commotion would surely wake her up.

By eleven in the morning, I walked into her room with a cup of coffee. I had seen her shifting around in bed. I already knew that if she was not feeling well enough, she'd begin telling me how something hurt, but she didn't. She slowly pulled herself into a sitting position and thanked me for the coffee. Her hands were trembling slightly. She stretched one arm, the other arm, her neck, and finally sat on the side of the bed. "Breakfast is ready, Mija. I'm ready too. Go clean up and hurry as I want to go to the stores as early as possible. I don't want to come back here when it's dark." She drank a little bit of coffee and walked to the bathroom. She spent at least thirty minutes in the bathroom. She would do that quite a bit during the daytime. All those pills were causing her to have constipation lately. Darn pills! I thought. I knew well enough how doctors tend to overmedicate their patients here in the United States. I mean, after all, they usually get kickbacks from the pharmaceutical companies. I wish Maxi would just start weaning herself off of many of those pills, but she was still in that haze I knew all too well. The fact that we were going on a shopping spree was a big step forward.

By close to one PM, we were finally off to the shopping area all the way to Austin. The whole time, Maxi kept looking at houses to purchase. Unfortunately, the housing market was out of control. There was no way she would be able to buy a house with the amount of money she had received from the divorce, but it was good that she was looking at the future and not the past. "Oh my God, mom! This one is beautiful! That pool in the backyard! I could do my physical therapy there instead of wasting all that money on physical therapy! I know I want a place with a pool because that would help me. I love swimming." She was chatty, which was a really good sign.

"Mom, I was wondering about all of your past, and how did you ever survive all that? I would have likely killed myself or would have run away."

"Ay Mija, what is it to be well put together? I don't believe that a single human being in this world has not had to deal with 'issues.'"

We continued talking about her future. But, of course, I will never understand all this obsession over social internet forums. I truly believe our society is kidding itself, and we kid each other. Sometimes I secretly wish for the internet to be taken down permanently.

"You're right, mom. I mean, I have several friends who already have two divorces. They never put it on their Facebook accounts all the drama. All they do is change their status to single and soon after to in a relationship. I had never thought of that."

Everyone I know is worried about their Facebook page and their status. I honestly believe that our children and our young parents have bought into this mentality. If you are trying to improve yourself, don't fear society. Do right by you. Think about your journey and where you are now, and focus on yourself. Leave behind this attention and validation-seeking mentality we have grown to be part of. It's not a healthy thing to live by.

This type of behavior leads us to second guess ourselves or find the wrong type of 'team' to support us. It's no wonder many young adults fall prey to the many extremists out there. We want to belong so badly that we lose sight of reality. If you aren't in the right team, people are likely to shit on you and your life story. I say let them. Ignore them.

Don't be afraid to come back out and speak your truth.

We arrived at our first store. JCPenney. I loved shopping at JCPenney, and I had been a customer of theirs all my life. Maxi went off to find some things, and I went off to the lady's department. I could see her looking at shirts and began trying some things. It was very frustrating for both of us to find clothing that fit us just right. I had the biggest boobs in the family, and she had thick upper arms that she hated. Finally, I found the same old style of shirts that I knew fit me and would stretch if my boobs decided to grow more. I was already a triple D size the last time I bought new bras, but I made sure Maxi found some nice-looking clothes that fit her right. I could see she was having fun. There was a lightness in her step. After three hours of jumping from store to store, we were quite exhausted. "Hey, let's go somewhere nice to eat," I said

"Ay, Mami, I'm super tired. How about we pick up something?" I looked over at her, and yes, she looked like shit. She had walked more than she had walked in months.

"OK." We picked up something very unhealthy and began making our way back to the little town. I had bought that little house that was still needing lots of updates, but it was fully paid for, and so it was mine. On our way back home, Maxi was very quiet. She was not eating much, and I wondered if I had pushed her too hard.

"Are you OK, Mija? Why aren't you eating?"

"I'm OK, mom. It's just that I'm super tired. I need to first smoke to get hungry or eat one of those CBD gummies," she said. Some of the medications she was under caused her not to be hungry or have nausea. "Want me to stop in one of those CBD places to pick up some gummies?" "Yes, please." "Look for the closest one to us." So we made our way to a CBD store and bought several of those gummies. She took one and got back into the car. After a short while, she began eating. She passed me my burger, and I ate as I drove. It was a long drive, and the sun was already beginning to slide into the horizon. The beautiful colors in the sky made me sigh. They reminded me of the wonderful colors from Qatar when the sun went down. Of course, the Qatar sunsets were more beautiful than this one, but this one was close enough.

"Mija, look at the sunset. It's beautiful, don't you think?"

"Oh yeah, mom! Look at those orange colors!" she said with excitement. The CBD had done its job. She was in happy dope-landia. I did not mind at all. I had changed my mind about marijuana when faced with one of my many health issues. The doctor himself told me I had to consume marijuana or I would not make it to the operating table. At the time, I was dating this man who turned out to be a consumer of marijuana, and he was excited to hear this. Thus, my induction into that world began.

"Hey Maxi, do you remember when I had to consume marijuana? I was what, around forty?" I said to her. She loved talking about my induction into the marijuana world. "I was afraid I would die before that really hard operation."

"What was wrong with you when that happened?"

I had some tumors and strands wrapped around my large intestine and other parts of my insides. The tumors were benign, but the damage the strands were causing on my insides was no less serious. The strands of the tumor were attached to my right hip and bones, so when I moved in certain ways, I feel felt this awful tearing inside me. I'd stop, take a deep breath, and wait for the pain to be over. For years, I had told doctors something was wrong with my uterus and my ovaries. When they looked inside, they'd say that there was nothing wrong with me and that I had one large ovary, but it looked fine.

"You know all the vomiting I used to have?" I said. "Well, it was caused by the strands from the tumor wrapped around my intestine. I don't know how many times I landed in the hospital, and every single time, the nurses and doctors would check me and say there was nothing wrong with me. But, you know, Mija, God sends you people into your life when you need them."

My boyfriend's mom was a nurse, and one of those times that I ended up in the hospital bent over with pain, someone told him I was an addict. He got so mad because he knew I was far from that. He got his mom on the phone and got the staff to get a move on with me. They did another MRI with contrast. Lo and behold, my right ovary had been pushed between my large intestine. That likely happened due to the sexual abuse when I was a child. A tumor had grown where the ovary should have been. By all accounts, and according to the doctors, it looked just like my ovary. I call it my ghost ovary. That day they told me I had to have an operation as urgently as possible. However, I was on full disability receiving Medicare, and there's no such thing as an urgent operation for Medicare.

The Medicare folks took their sweet time to approve the operation and pushed the date into the future to the point that the doctor that was seeing me told me I would not make it to the operation table if I waited that long. The pain had become unbearable. They'd given me morphine, and that did not do shit with the pain. It only put me in a stupor. I hate that feeling. My boyfriend got some marijuana somewhere and began making food with it trying to get me to eat anything.

"That's why I was so thin, Mija. I weighed like ninety pounds at the time," I said.

I still ended up in the ER room at least two more times before I figured out that the best method for me was to just make a tea and drink it as quickly as possible so that it would take effect and the swelling in my intestine would go down. The doctors kept asking me if I had had children. One doctor commented that he could not fathom how my insides were the way they were.

"You know Maxi, you three were God sent. He meant for you to be here with me. A miracle, nonetheless. Once they removed the tumor, the ovaries, and my uterus, most of my health problems went away. Now I have fatty person problems," I said, laughing. Look at me! "I'm a chunky sort of healthy, strong feminazi!"

"We are strong feminazis, mom!" Maxi said, pushing another french fry in her mouth.

Maxi and I were able to laugh about it then because I never knew how bad my situation was. There are two ways to look at this. On the one hand, this is kind of how miracles work. You don't always know you've been blessed until the most critical moment. I was very blessed.

On the other hand, it's not uncommon for abuse survivors to underestimate the severity of their condition. It's not always about PTSD. Sometimes, survivors have built such a tolerance they don't recognize when they are under intense pressure or harm.

I was more grateful than ever to have my daughters after that incident because it was miraculous, according to the doctors. I was also so proud to be with Maxi then. She had come so far. Yes, we had gotten on each other's nerves, but a mother's love never leaves their child. I will always be proud of my girls—all three of them. This book (this chapter of life) is about saving Maxi from the brink of destruction when evil was after her. Still, I want to say that I would be there for all of my girls just the same if they ever need me and allow me to.

"Mija, do you know how proud I am of you?" I said. "I'm so proud of you! You have taken a terrible situation and look at you now. You are beginning to claim the feminazi crown."

She smiled and said, "Well, I have the mother feminazi to learn from." My girl was going to be alright. She was beginning to talk about the future, and we had just gone on our first of several shopping sprees. She was beginning to laugh more. She sang along to one of my happy songs when we pulled into the driveway. It was a full moon night, and I told her. "Look at that beautiful full moon! Let's drop the bags in the house and sit out here. The dogs need to come out anyway." We sat in silence, looking at the sky. Silently, I thanked God that she had turned yet another corner.

Weeks went by, and she began going out more and more. She'd go to the store to pick up groceries or drive to Austin for doctor appointments. She came home with a shirt or a pair of pants she had found in a store and was so eager to show me. I was so blessed to have her and her sisters in my life.

Then the time came when she had become strong enough to move on. She had found a place closer to Austin. She had not found her forever home but had decided to rent a two-bedroom trailer. Rental prices were out of control, but she had found that place all by herself. She hired movers, and she flew away like a little bird. Off she went to begin another chapter in her life. She had so many plans now that I could not keep up with them. Her smile was full and not forced. It was a true smile of happiness. I was eager to have my house of my own again and to see her become the woman I knew she could be.

You too will be alright. I know it, and so do you.

CHAPTER 11

HAPPY TIMES

Around a year after the divorce, Maxi was almost her old self. It was remarkable o think because many women struggle to heal for so much longer. I was already hoping she was dating again. I suppose I moved a little faster than her because whenever I asked about that, she'd say she wasn't ready. She had begun to hang out with her sisters and some old friends though.

At first, she told me, it was weird because she felt as if they were being too critical of her. I gave my girls the same advice. "Come on, girls. You need to get along! Try to hear each other out and not jump to conclusions or cut each other down. I don't understand why women do that to each other. You don't want to be like that. Come on, I taught you better than that."

I'd get emoji's that were sighing or crying, but somehow I knew my girls would be fine. My oldest was an amazing woman already. She had done so much in life that anytime I talked about her, I'd beam with pride. Now my second girl would surely follow suit. My baby girl had gotten married and was following in her older sister's steps.

We still talked almost every day. I was feeling uneasy about all the man-hating conversations we had so often that I decided it was time for Maxi to hear about my dad. I barely, if ever, talked about him. My girls knew I loved him dearly as I had dedicated a poem to him a year after he had passed away.

In one of Maxi's visits she was contemplating the poem. Reading it out loud:

"Ashes"

You are the ashes of this earth
that holds you deep in it.
You were a man that had a dream
that felt it very deep.

You are in every memory
that I hold in my heart.
You were my guide and guiding light
that showed me when to part.

You are the love that grows in me
that never shall forget.
You were a simple humble man
that knew not to regret.

*You are the ashes of this earth
that I hold deep in me.
You were and still are in my heart
that forgets not of thee.*

After she finished reading, she asked me what it meant to me, why I wrote it. I explained to her that I had written that poem when I was maybe eighteen or nineteen. I won an Editor's Choice Award for it. I told her about my dad. The kind quiet gentle giant that went to heaven way too early. He was only fifty-two when he passed away. Cancer took him. She asked why I rarely ever talked about him. I explained that there was nothing much I could say about him other than the kind human being he was. Men like him are long gone, I think. He treated my mother like a queen. Anything she wanted she got.

For years I suffered humiliation from my family as according to them I was dad's favorite daughter and hence spoiled rotten by him. I never tell him about the sexual abuse because I knew him too well. I was afraid he'd end up in jail because I could see him killing his own son. That's what stopped me. You see, my dad and Will didn't get along that well and he blamed my mother for the alcoholic Willy became.

As for the other brothers and sisters, dad did show preference for Roland and Lewy. Roland was the youngest of all of us. In fact, he was only six when dad passed away. Eight years younger than me. But, when it came to Lewy, dad went all out. He truly showed him how much he cared about him. Dad gleamed with pride as he saw his boy join a football team. A game he knew nothing at all but learned as he dragged us all to the football games every Friday night. The day Lewy scored a touchdown and his name came over the intercom, dad's smile was the biggest smile I had ever seen. He'd tell people around him, "That's my son, the one that made the touchdown!" I truly believe my brother Lewy was born with all the alignments of every star and planet.

Unfortunately, like I said, dad died when I was fourteen. That year, 1981, was the hardest year that our family endured. My mother would go off to work and was gone for long hours and days at times while Lewy and my sister Mimi would do the same just to try and cover medical bills and any other needs that we had in our family. I stayed home during that summer. I saw my dad shrink from a six-foot tall, muscular man into nearly nothing. I swear at fourteen, I could carry him and I cared for him as honorably and as best as I could.

I don't like remembering those sad days, but I will tell you that my dad was one of the most honorable men I knew. We worked in the fields and we were not treated all that well, even though my father had made it a point to make sure that when we migrated to the United States, we did so legally. Still, people were very racist back than but more so toward illegals.

One day, I was told by my older brothers and sisters, one of the hand man from a ranch we were working on, decided he'd beat the shit out of this scrawny illegal Mexican man. In front of all the workers, he began beating the shit out of him. When the man was clearly barely able to stay up, my dad stepped in. In broken English my dad told the hand man that if he continued that he'd make sure to call the cops on him because no human being deserved that kind of treatment. If it was not for dad, that poor man would have been murdered.

Most times during weekends we would work the fields in Texas. We'd stand out at the Workforce Commission Office and trucks would drive by asking for workers to work the fields. On one occasion we were promised a specific payment, but once we got there, the man that took us to their land said he had decided to pay us much less. My dad stood in front of everyone and said to that man, "What, are you not a real man? You don't know how to keep your word so you must not be a real man?" back then, keeping your word was still a big deal. So, once that happened my dad told us we had to walk back home.

Eventually, walking down that same road we saw other workers in a different farm and we were hired there. We actually made much more money than if we would have stayed at the other place. There's one last bit of information I want readers to know. My dad and my older brothers marched with Cesar Chavez. I'm very sure it was dad who encouraged others to do this as it was the only way to bring change to what can only be described as cruel treatment of human beings. My dad was an honorable man. The kind that mean what they say and say what they mean. The kind that don't complain about the amount of work they have to do just to feed ten kids and a wife. In my solitude I pray that my girls find this kind of man.

Months passed by and I was hopeful that Maxi would find her special someone. Then it happened. The day she said she was dating was one of the happiest days of my life. She had gotten back on the love saddle. Apparently, there was this guy who I knew and she was feeling happy.

"Mom, you have been so right about so many things. I can't remember when I was this happy. I can't believe it took me so long to leave that bastard. I should have left him the moment he began abusing me. Never am I going to allow a man to step over that line. In fact mom, I would like you to meet the guy I'm dating. You know him from when we were in school." Her voice was beaming through the phone. I told her, well let's face time.

Mentally, I placed a prayer to God. "Please God, if this is the man for her, let things run smoothly and may he be patient with my girl. She needs a man that understands and accepts her as she is."

It was more than obvious that this man, Josh, was bringing joy into her life. That's all mothers ask for. We ask that our daughters be treated like queens because they are queens. We ask they be respected because they deserve to be respected. We ask that they be supported because they deserve support. We ask that they are loved as much as we love them.

That weekend my daughter came by to visit and in came Josh.

My girl had made it through. I knew that this life lesson was hers for ever and ever. She would one day pass it on to a friend or a daughter. Maybe even one of her sisters. As a mother, I was relieved. My girl was taking off. After all the troubles she had had with that awful ogre of a man, she had come out on the other side to be a strong feminazi. A woman that knows she has to be respected. She had learned from me how to respect but I had failed to teach her to require others to respect her.

Saturday came and here came the happy couple. They brought bags of gifts and ready-made food. They were beaming with love and happiness. My heart skipped as I remembered that feeling. I quickly ignored it because at my age, that was the last thing on my mind.

As families do, she began to show him all the albums. Then she began to brag about me. My accomplishments in acting and such.She begged me to share all my accomplishments and travels as well. Poor guy, he must have been bored out of his mind. But he was polite and patient. Two qualities I like.

I thought about the many things I had endured and celebrated in my life. The many chapters and I prayed I had made an everlasting impact on my girls so that they too could go out there and chase their dreams. It is here that I tell some of my readers that there's hope. I know that if you are in the midst of a divorce you may feel there isn't such a thing. I know that if you are dealing with any type of abuse, you might feel there isn't hope for you. But my family is proof of the resilience within us and within you too.

We had a wonderful Saturday lunch and before the sun began to head set, they left. The smell of love and happiness lingered in my house for days. I could not help but to smile about the whole ordeal. Yup, we were feminazi and proud of it!

CHAPTER 12

REFLECTIONS

As Maxi and Josh continued to look at albums, Maxi pointed to an old picture, wondering who those people were. I sat with them, telling her how we used to go up to the northern states as a family to work in the fields. The stories I shared about all those trips filled the air with excitement, laughter, and at times sadness. You see, even though my life was as it was, as a family, we did have many wonderful moments.

Like the time my parents had bought a green trunk trailer. My parents needed it to carry all the supplies and clothing from state to state. That trailer truck has been in our happy conversations because, on at least two occasions, it ended up getting unhitched as we were going down a hill. One of those times, my brother Jay turned to look out the window, and he said to my parents, "Hey, isn't that our trailer!" as we watched the trailer keep going down the hill past our station wagon. When it neared the bottom of the hill, Jay jumped out of the station wagon and began chasing it. His long skinny legs could not stop the trailer, so another brother, Lewy, jumped out and did the same. Eventually, the trailer truck came to a stop, but my brothers and sisters would laugh hysterically when they remembered that ordeal.

Then there was the time when my mother got sick while we were working in the fields. My mother used to wear her underwear, pantyhose, and a girdle belt. Apparently, she kept eating hot peach as we picked it, and dad had told her not to eat the fruit when it was hot because she would get sick. It wasn't long before we saw her rushing to the outskirts of the field with my oldest sister in tow. Before she could pull off her clothes... well... According to my older sister, the smell was so bad that she ended up gagging and vomiting. Mother, behaving like a little girl, began calling my sister 'manita', which is an endearment for a best friend or a sister and not for a daughter. She told my sister, "Come on. Please help me, manita. Just pull on the pantyhose, manita."

We laughed until we had tears in our eyes and our stomachs hurt.

I'm not telling you these stories because I don't want to end my book on a crappy story. I'm telling them because, if nothing else, they are reminders that even in the darkest of times, light can be found. More importantly, as we grow, we can choose the memories we want to keep and use them to tell our stories. Yes, my mom did cruel things. My family abandoned me in a time of need.

But at some points, we were family, and perhaps these stories are a part of the key to our healing.

It is moments like this one that I hold in my heart. Glimpses of laughter and happiness. Even though they were not that many, these are the moments that I chose to remember my family by. Maybe, just maybe, reminding everyone in my family that these are the moments we need to remember and not the sad moments. I hope this will bring some form of healing.

No matter what you're going through or have been through, your story is yours. It's OK to hurt, to cry, to be angry. It's OK if you aren't ready to forgive and don't know if you ever will be. I'm not here to tell you what to do. Like my Maxi, you have to live your life. But also, like her, you have me—my stories—to remind you to get back up. To keep going. You are not alone, and you are not crazy. Life gets hard, but you have strength. We women all do. (Yeah, I'm the Feminazi who said women are strong!)

Abuse, no matter who it comes from, does not have to define you. It is not the end of your story. I hope that the stories I've shared from my past and Maxi's journey help you to see the bigger picture and to know what to do when faced with an emotional crisis. There's a reason this book is titled Hose the House Down. It's from an old habit my mom had. She would grab the hose and bring it through a window or the door and hose down everything in the kitchen and living room.

It sounds crazy, but I thought it was the perfect metaphor for the resilience she had when things got impossibly hard at home. Sometimes things in your life won't make sense. Sometimes the house is your mind, and things are so out of place because your life seems to be crumbling around you. All you can do is renew your mind by taking one seemingly crazy step at a time. It's your house. Clean it how you want to.

Acknowledgments

Writing a book has been something I've planned on for a very long time. Every time someone has heard my stories, they've told me I have many books in me. It's been a long time coming. I wouldn't have this moment now (hopefully the first of many) if it weren't for the support of some truly key people, whom I would like to acknowledge here.

First, I'd like to thank my friend and colleague, Cynthia. I was talking with my daughter about finally writing one day soon, and as if God heard me (He did), Cynthia called me and made a connection for me with someone she was sure could help me. Thank you, Cynthia.

Second, I'd like to thank my editor. He's been so patient and honest and caring in hearing my story. This process of working together to gather my thoughts and turn them into something I can see and hold and share has been nothing short of amazing. Thank you for all you do!

Next, my brother Rolando and my sister-in-law Sonia. I want to thank them for always being there when my girls or I needed them. As you may now know, family has been a bit of a tempestuous word for me, but they have been a constant source of love and support. Thank you for being my family.

Last but not least, I must thank my daughter, Maxi, for allowing me to champion her through one of the toughest times in her life and for giving us a chance to heal, learn, and tighten our bond.

To all of my daughters. Remember, I still love the three of you equally! (You can envision me raising my eyebrow, with my hands on my hips if you want.) Know that if you're ever in any kind of crisis, and if you allow me to, I will be there for you.

This book couldn't be what it is without any of you. Thank you!

—Shelly

About the Author

Araceli Vasquez was born into a migrant family in the late 1960s. Daughter of a carpenter and a housewife, Araceli was the seventh of ten children. Survivor of extreme abuse as both a child and later as a married woman, Araceli has become a beacon of strength and support for survivors of abuse. Her life experiences are valuable for anyone.

As a young adult, Araceli sought a degree in Psychology only to later go into Elementary Education. Having taught hundreds of children the fine art of kindness and empathy, she has now decided that it's time to tell her story in a series of books. As a published poet, several of her poems ended up as Spanish songs.

She is the mother of three adult daughters, whom she loves dearly and equally. Writing this book, for her, was an opportunity to leave a little something behind of her legacy and relationship with them. She believes in the strength of women and the importance of mothers helping daughters to become confident and capable. She is also an advocate for men's mental health, as she believes it is a crucial piece to ending cycles of abuse.

Araceli is a career-long educator and has worked as a teacher around the globe. She returned to the United States to be close to her daughters, but looks forward to traveling again some day.